MEMORIES OF A WAYFARING MAN

REV. MURDOCH CAMPBELL

WM 1

Printed by
HIGHLAND PRINTERS LTD.,
Diriebught Road.
Inverness.

CONTENTS

INTRODUCTION

ONE EVENING, a number of years ago, a friend suggested that I should sometime write a brief account of my spiritual pilgrimage. I had, in fact, before that time kept my own memory refreshed by writing down recollections which I could not but prize. The following pages, therefore, tell a little of the story of God's mercy and love which so many of His people could also tell. As to the propriety of unfolding some of God's dealings with one's spirit, it is enough to say that in the past many Christian ministers and people felt impelled to do this.

In giving these memories the writer's only motive is to magnify the grace of God, and to encourage God's people, many of whom, "in the footsteps of the flock," carry heavy burdens and are often weary and afraid on the way. For that reason, also, I have refrained from saying much about my public work.

The somewhat "mystic" vein which runs through my story I thought of suppressing, but on second thoughts I decided to let it stand. This I did because it is, as I hope, something wholly related to the inspired Word of God.

When Doctor John Kennedy wrote his well-known book, "The Days of the Fathers in Ross-shire," he anticipated some adverse criticisms of its contents from some who might disapprove of those anecdotes which tell of strange and unusual experiences of some of God's people. We know, however, that he wrote nothing out of harmony with God's inerrant Word and with true Christian experience. I hope I could also, and in all humility, say the same of what I have related in these pages.

Murdoch Campbell.

Resolis, Ross-shire.

Chapter One

AN EARLY BLESSING

ONE DAY, at the beginning of this century, a young mother could be seen leading a small boy by the hand along a narrow Hebridean road. They reach a cottage into which they enter very quietly. They are welcomed in a subdued voice by another young woman. As they enter, their eyes turn instinctively towards the bed in a corner of the room. The aged woman in the bed looks towards the company. Seeing "the child" for whom she had so urgently sent, she asks that he might be brought beside her. With her frail hand resting on his head she solemnly invoked the blessing of the Triune God on his life. Then, after a few fervent words of prayer to "the Beloved" that the "wheels of His chariot" should no longer tarry, she yielded up her spirit into God's strong hand.

So ended the earthly life of Margaret Campbell. So also began the life of that child whose eyes must have seen her before she passed into Heaven, but whose memory holds no recollection of that — to me — precious hour. Margaret Campbell was my grandmother, and I was the unconscious recipient of the blessing which God had promised her for me. Of this incident my parents told me time and again.

Margaret Campbell knew the Lord from her early years. When her parents, with the rest of the family, sailed for the more hopeful shores of the 'New World,' she refused to accompany them. To those who entreated her to leave her native island for a land where her earthly life might prosper she would speak of those who, in other ages, chose rather to suffer affliction with the people of God than to enjoy earthly comforts. Her reluctance to leave her native land was really due to her spiritual attachment to a pious but blind relative to whom she had become "eyes" as she went from place to place seeking the Bread of Life. Denied light, Margaret's young hand was this aged woman's unfailing guide.

One year they both travelled the long distance to Uig. Like the rest of Lewis, God's Spirit had been poured out in abundance on that favoured parish a few years before. "The shout of a King" was among the multitudes who gathered there at Communion seasons to worship the Lord. "Angus of the hills," the weak and illiterate, but Heaven-blessed man, was there that Sabbath. Angus had become a "wonder to many" by reason of his wonderful conversion and sanctified life. As the large open-air congregation was in the act of dispersing he took his "blind sister" by the hand and together they sang a joyous Psalm. Neither the astonished people nor the embarrassed Margaret could do anything but watch a scene which must have brought tears to many eyes.

A few hours before this good woman left the world she said to her devoted niece: "Come, Margaret, for I have news for you. The Lord has promised that 'it shall be well with thy remnant.'" (Jer. 15, 11). This promise the Lord graciously fulfilled. Not only was Margaret herself provided with a husband who was both gifted and gracious, but her family also came to the knowledge of the Lord. They all witnessed a good confession before leaving this world. Their mother's consecrated and prayerful life made a lasting impression on them all.

There were many, indeed, outside the circle of her own family who were deeply impressed by her holiness of life, and by her nearness to the Lord. A young girl who sometimes shared her lone shieling during the summer months used to repeat the spontaneous verses which fell from her lips, and which expressed her longing to be with Christ. One of these was about the "brooks of honey" which shall nourish and delight "the poor and needy" in the heavenly Canaan.

There was also a young man in the district who used to tell the story of a stormy day at sea when a local boat had to leave the fishing ground without lifting its lines. A day or two afterwards, when the storm had abated, an anxious member of the crew consulted her about the propriety of going to look for the lines. "You may go," she said, "for there is a smile on the face of the Lord in His providence." Later they found their fishing lines in perfect order, along with welcome tokens of God's goodness.

Her eldest son died suddenly in the fulness of his strength and in the prime of his life. The night on which he died his wife observed that at worship he quoted in his native Gaelic the Paraphrase which begins with the words:

> "My race is run; the warfare's o'er;
> The solemn hour is nigh,
> When offered up to God my soul
> Shall wing its flight on high."

A few moments afterwards he sank to the floor and died. Another son died at the age of twenty-four. His last whispered words on earth were — "Christ is sweet, sweet, sweet . . ."

But of all the family, John we believe, was the one who lived nearest to the Lord. John's most marked characteristic was his love of solitude. The barn, where he daily prayed, he called his 'Divinity Hall.' His almost constant enjoyment of God's presence wrought in him, in his latter years, such a degree of assurance of God's love as made all dubiety with respect to his personal salvation quite depart from his mind. If some of his friends looked upon the grace of an unclouded assurance as a very rare Christian attainment, he refused to trim his sails to suit the views of those who travelled under skies less bright than his own. Rather than cast any reflection on the goodness and the love of the Redeemer he was not slow to confess that his lines had fallen in a pleasant place. If John began his course as a Christian with 'the wind contrary,' the Lord gave him at the end a clear sunset on a calm sea. He left this world singing a verse from a psalm.

> "They shall be brought with gladness great,
> And mirth on every side,
> Into the palace of the King;
> And there they shall abide." (Ps. 45)

As the last word died on his lips he was here no more. He was wafted into Heaven on a wave of joy.

My father, Alexander Campbell, began to seek the Lord while he was still a mere lad. The Rev. Duncan MacBeath was the man God used to show him he was a sinner under wrath. This was followed by a season of mental anguish and deep conviction of sin. One evening his mother advised him to attend a local meeting of prayer. That night his burdened soul found rest in these words: "I, even I am He that blotteth out thy transgressions for Mine Own sake, and will not remember thy sins." Returning from a service soon afterwards his heart was so full of the consolations of God that, instead of going home, he decided to tarry for a while in a lonely hollow near the shore where he might commune with his Redeemer. The Lord, on that occasion, however, proved to be as a 'Way-faring man.' Surprised and saddened that with the dawn of his faith came also its cloud, he called that evening on an eminent Christian woman in his native village. He told her his sad story of how he had lost so soon what he had hoped to retain a while. She comforted him by saying that only twice in her life did she enjoy such an overflowing measure of the love of Christ as he had enjoyed that day.

Shortly afterwards he walked many miles across the moor looking for stray sheep. It was winter. As he sat down to rest for a moment he suddenly found himself on the fringe of another world. He lost all consciousness both of time and of his immediate surroundings. That day the Lord revealed to his soul the excelling beauty of His own perfections, and the preciousness of those spiritual truths which had now become his inheritance. The glorious spiritual world which he had just entered he saw by faith. The glory of Christ, and His way of salvation, were also presented to him in a fuller light! Melted down under the abundance of the revelation he could only bless his God.

A little while afterwards a young God-fearing companion, Donald Murray, Swainbost, found him apparently forgetful that night was falling. On the way home he repeatedly quoted the words: "Blessed art thou, Simon, Barjona, for flesh and blood hath not revealed it unto thee, but my Father Who is in Heaven." He could never look back on "that good day" without being both affected and solemnised. It was one of his Bethel hours.

My father used to tell of another incident which happened shortly after his conversion. There was in his native village an old and enfeebled Christian woman who accompanied another young man and himself to attend a Communion in the vicinity of Stornoway. After walking over fourteen miles this aged woman lost all power to go on. On the lonely moorland road they sat down and prayed for help. Soon a cart appeared on the scene, but although it was quite empty, the gruff man who owned it refused to help. He had not gone forward many yards, however, before the animal shied violently, till both horse and cart were quite bogged in the soft moorland. Every effort to coax it forward failed. The young men, who meantime watched the man's struggle with the animal, rebuked him for his refusal to help one of God's fainting children. They reminded him of how a dumb ass once rebuked the madness of a prophet. At this stage the exasperated man was willing to try any experiment to get out of his predicament. "We shall let this woman sit in the cart," counselled my father's friend, "and if the horse still refuses to move forward God's hand is not in the matter, but if it does you are meant to take her." No sooner was she seated in the cart than the horse heaved itself out of the bog and walked away in perfect docility.

On another occasion, and on the way to Communion services with several companions, they overtook an old woman. This eminently godly woman was known throughout the island as "Eirig Ruadh," from the village of Bragar. The way was long and the good woman was leaning on the arm of a younger friend. They had not seen her before, so that they passed her by without speaking. They had hardly moved in front of her, however, than she cried, "How is it that my Father's children pass me in the way without speaking?" When they turned round to acknowledge her salutation she earnestly looked into their faces. Then addressing one of the party she said. "When I spoke of my Father's children I did not mean you, for I fear you are not one of them." The person concerned was then showing much apparent interest in spiritual things. The time came, however, when she sank back into her former ways of spiritual unconcern. And, as far as man could judge, in that state she left the world.

My mother also knew the Lord. Of a retiring disposition she lingered long on the threshold of "the Heavenly Mansion" before venturing in. During one Communion season she prayed for strength to make a public confession of her faith. The preliminary services passed and she was still unable to see her minister and the session.

On the Sabbath morning, as she saw some of God's people walking in front of her toward the Church, the words, "Who are these that fly as a cloud and as the doves to their windows?" came with great power to her mind. They also warmed her heart. Her hesitancy vanished, and the minister and his elders whom she saw before the service gave her permission to sit at the Lord's Table with His people.

What I particularly remember about my parents was their deep spiritual sympathy the one with the other. As heirs together of the grace of life, they walked by the same rule and minded the same things. As a comment on this inner harmony and sympathy between them let me relate one other incident. On one occasion my father was much troubled over a vain and silly song which kept repeating itself within his mind. All this he kept to himself. Then to his amazement he heard my mother's voice quoting a verse of that very song. "Woman," he said to her, "what has gone wrong with you?" She then remarked that having repeated the verse, the unwelcome intruder, which, against his will, kept invading his mind, would trouble him no more. And so it was.

The night my mother died in the Spring of 1931, I awoke out of sleep with the cry of "Mother" on my lips. The cry, as if charged through with a great sorrow, awoke my wife also. Before I awoke I seemed to see her in a dream leaving the earth wrapped in what appeared to be a luminous cloud which swiftly passed out of sight in the sky. This vivid dream coincided with what I knew, even in my sleep, to be my last sight of her in this world. It was exactly four in the morning. Several hours later word reached us at Fort Augustus that she had passed away at that very hour.

Nearly all her married life an invalid, she left this world quoting the words, "For I reckon that the sufferings of the present time are not worthy to be compared with the glory which shall be revealed in us."

CHAPTER TWO

MY FIRST PRAYER

ONE OF my earliest memories is that of standing before my father lisping a prayer which he wanted me to repeat every day till the Lord would give me a prayer from Himself. For a mere child beginning to put words together this prayer was not only a light burden, but also a suitable plea.

"Lord, in mercy open the eyes of my soul that I may see my need of Christ. Amen."

That was all. This prayer was so woven into my mind and memory that for some years, without adding to it or taking from it, I said it night and day, both on rising and on lying down to sleep.

Another precious memory is that of awakening betimes in the early morning and hearing my Father's voice in secret prayer in another room. I used to wonder at the long time he took to "say his prayers" while I could get through mine in less than half a minute! It was often that musical, earnest voice when I awoke, and the accents of it which would frequently die away as I sank into sleep again.

Occasionally my father, as an elder of the Church, was asked to pray with the sick and the dying. One night he had been asked to pray at the bedside of a dying woman in the district. But no words could he utter. His lips were sealed, and his mind was so disturbed and imprisoned that he fled from a place which he felt was darkened by the shadow of Evil.

On another evening, as I remember, he arrived home in a state of great joy. He had been visiting a dying lad, Angus Mackay by name, who lived in the village of Skigersta. This young man, already on the threshold of heaven, and enraptured at the prospect of presently seeing his Redeemer, bade him a fond farewell and, as a last request, had asked him to read at family worship that chapter in the Song of Solomon which contains the words: "The voice of my Beloved! behold He cometh . . . . "

Twice a day family worship was observed in our home, and as my father was gifted with an excellent tenor voice the singing of a Gaelic Psalm made this hour of devotion pleasant, even to a child.

One of our little innocent pastimes on the Lord's Day was to sit in a corner by the window and watch the huge concourse of people who passed by to Church services. A little after eleven a lone old woman would appear on the Habost Brae followed by several others whose age demanded that they should walk slowly in the way. These were followed by a growing trickle of some who were not so old, but who had made a becoming habit of arriving at God's house in good time.

Then the trickle, like a river suddenly in spate, would grow in volume as a procession of men and women of all ages marched by. The day and the occasion were held in deep reverence. The men never smoked on their way to Church, and what conversation was engaged in was carried on in a subdued voice. After a quarter of an hour or so the last of the people ("an sluagh") would disappear over the crest of the village brae leaving the whole parish under the mantle of a great silence.

In our home, as in the local school, the Shorter Catechism was next to the Bible, our spiritual guide. Little did I know in those early years what the questions and answers of that comprehensive and precious little book really meant; but the day came when I could rejoice that this — to use a metaphor — spiritual gold was put into my purse, when as yet I knew but little of its true value. Those who, in this age, say that the teachings of the Catechism are too difficult and obtuse for mere children, should realise that what goes into the mind by the door of memory in our early days is often that which shapes our character in after life. And since this little book contains the pure seed of God's Word, its teachings, by the blessing of God, have often led many into the path that leads to eternal life.

I well remember one of my first visits to Church. In the pulpit was a white-haired, vigorous old minister, Mr Rose of Lochs, who preached on the words; "Awake thou that sleepest, and arise from the dead, and Christ shall give thee light." Judging by the frequency with which he repeated these words, his sermon must have been an appeal to the people of God to maintain their spiritual vigilance, and to the sinner to forsake his spiritual grave and come to Christ for salvation. But what left the deepest impression on my mind that evening was the volume and exquisite quality of the Gaelic singing. To me, the nearest approach to the song of the Redeemed within the veil in the upper world, was our Highland Psalm-singing in the days when God's Spirit, like a warm living wind, moved the hearts of those large gatherings which met to praise God in His Zion.

The wave of spiritual power which swept over Lewis in the great revival of 1818-1829 has, in fact, not yet spent itself. Although we live in a day "when the enemy is come in like a flood." God is still working among this people. My frequent visits to my native island have left me with the conviction and the consolation that "The Lord is there."

During one of my visits to Lewis, for example, I was told of an incident which revealed how deeply the Word of God had touched the inner life of many of the inhabitants. It happened, as I remember, in the autumn of 1939 when the war crisis had compelled the mobilization of our naval reserves. On that particular day, the town of Stornoway observed the Fast Day which preceded the local Communion services. Moving towards the pier that day were nearly a thousand young men who were about to leave their native shore for war service. These crowded into the waiting ship, while many friends stood near to say a fond farewell to their relatives, sweethearts and friends. A great silence fell on the crowd.

The day was devoted to the worship of God, and hearts were too sad and too full for mere words. Then it happened. A lone melodious voice began to sing verses from the forty sixth Psalm;

"God is our refuge and our strength;
In straits a present aid;
Therefore, although the earth remove
We will not be afraid."

The huge crowd took up the words till the sacred song gathered volume and wafted over the harbour and over the deserted streets of the town. This was not a display of feeling, but an expression of that trust in God which dwelt in many hearts. The vessel then left the shore and passed out of view, while the crowd, in silent little groups, moved away to their homes.

Looking back on those early days, I cannot but thank God that I was brought up in a community where, in the language of Scripture, God was well known and where His Name was great in the worship of His people. Some of the men and women whom I knew in those early days had a religion, the pure and vital springs of which arose from a deep personal experience of God's love and grace. They were a people who enjoyed much communion with God and to whom, therefore, the Eternal World was a living reality. Because God's grace reigned in their hearts they exhibited a nobility of bearing and tenderness of affection which the mere fashion of this world could never impart.

In my native parish of Ness, the people were blessed with a succession of Christian ministers upon whose labours the Lord set His seal. The minister of my boyhood days was the Rev. Duncan MacDougall, who was a native of Islay. Mr MacDougall was a man whose great intellectual powers were wedded to a kind and sympathetic heart. His exact knowledge of both ancient and modern languages gave his sermons an exegetical precision which greatly edified the large numbers of believers who waited on his words. Mr MacDougall was also one of my predecessors in Fort Augustus. Thereafter he laboured in Canada. In that land he was led into the path of controversy, and his terrible and unanswerable exposure of the idolatries and inconsistencies of Roman Catholicism often left his opponents silent and limp in his hands. His involvement in controversy, however, did not add to his comfort or popularity. The evening of his days he spent in his beloved Argyllshire where he laboured faithfully to the end.

Mr MacDougall's immediate successor in Ness was the much loved Mr Roderick John Macleod. This devoted servant of the Lord died in Dumbarton at the age of thirty-seven years. Ness was his first charge. He had hardly commenced his work there than signs began to multiply that God's Spirit was at work through his earnest and Scriptural preaching. A large number were brought out of darkness into light, and to the end of their days the lives and witness of those men and women showed that they were wrought in God.

Sometimes in the pulpit a small slip of paper could be seen in Mr Macleod's hand. On it were clearly marked the chapter and verse on which he was to base his theme. And thereby hangs a tale from his student days. It had to do with a strange dream and its remarkable sequel.

One night he dreamt that he was on his way to his native island and about to embark on a ship at Kyle of Lochalsh. But as the ship was engaged to carry servicemen only, he was compelled to sail in the other boat. When, in his dream, he at last reached his native shore he was horrified to see the other ship sinking in a rough sea and two of its sailor passengers struggling helplessly in the waves. These two he began to exhort earnestly to look to Christ for salvation before death would finally engulf them. Then he awoke.

Sometime after this he was preaching in the Partick Highland Mission in Glasgow. As the congregation were singing the Psalm which preceded the sermon he could not find his "text," which probably belonged to a different chapter to the one he had read. But at last, and in a state of much concern, he remembered his "dream" sermon and portion of Scripture on which it was based. That night the Lord blessed him with much spiritual freedom. After the service he was approached by two men, who, in soft broken voices, thanked him earnestly for a message which had led them to embrace the Saviour. And he recognised them as the two men to whom he had preached in his strange night vision. Shortly afterwards these two men, with many others, were drowned in the "Iolaire" disaster outside the Stornoway harbour. Truly God moves in a mysterious way.

Mr Macleod died in the full assurance of eternal life. His last words here were, "I am going to my God."

In my boyhood days there were many others in the community whose lives and Christian witness could not but command the interest and respect of all who value the ways of God. Of these I can only mention a few.

A man who, even now, I remember very vividly was John Murray, of Habost. John, who often visited our home, was a Christian man without guile. His warm sensitive spirit always kept him in the path of duty. One night after a day of toil in the deep — for he was a local fisherman — he came home very tired and ready to sleep. But deep down in his spirit he felt that if he went to bed there would be no one in the district keeping watch in prayer. For some time afterwards he remained in prayer that the Lord might watch over the land, and that the enemy of His glory might be restrained. After some time a voice seemed to say to him, "Now John, you may go to rest for your friend over in Skigersta is now on his knees." The next time these two worthy men met they each knew how the other was engaged on the night in question. So tender and near was the spiritual tie between them.

John had a neighbour whose name was John Macdonald. When word went round that John Macdonald was dying, his friends in the Lord gathered at his bedside to bid him a fond farewell and, in the words of Bunyan, 'to accompany him to the river.' A good man present, however, in a prayer that was heard in Heaven, asked the Lord to spare their friend for a while longer, as his prayers and witness were still needed in the community. From the gates of death the Lord raised this worthy man to shine again for a while in this lower vale as a light in a dark place.

A younger man than these was Donald Morrison of Eoropie. He was their equal, however, in ability and piety. Donald lived through the two great wars, and those who were out in the storms of those terrible years had a constant place in his prayers. So also had those on whose shoulders lay the burden of guiding the nation through its many perils. In this connection he used to tell of a certain night when after a season of prayer he retired to rest. And as he slept he dreamed. In this dream he saw a very alert-looking soldier who asked him to read from a Bible which he was holding in his hand. The portion of Scripture which he desired Donald to read was the sixty-eighth Psalm which begins with the words: "Let God arise, and let His enemies be scattered." Donald read the Psalm, after which he handed the Book to the soldier. Shortly afterwards news came that the British

Forces had attacked the German army, and that on General Montgomery's instructions, the battle-cry of the armies of Britain was the exact words quoted above. Donald carried such a vivid impression of the soldier of his dream that when he afterwards saw a picture of him he immediately recognised him as General Montgomery of Alamein. And, as I remember, he had never seen the likeness of the famous soldier before.

There was another eminent Christian man in my native village who commanded the deep respect of all the Lord's people. He was Malcolm MacLeod who, over the years, was the main pillar in the local Free Presbyterian Church. Malcolm's grasp of God's Word, and his edifying comments on Scripture were both comprehensive and profound. He was a man whom my father deeply revered and, like many others in the island, the bond between them was one of sincere and abiding Christian affection.

Another remarkable man who moved in the religious circles of those days was Norman Macdonald of Galson. Widely known throughout the Island as "Happy Norman," this excellent man lived a life of almost constant communion with the Lord. He walked with the Angel of the Covenant as with a Friend. Like Asaph of old, he could say,

> "Nevertheless continually,
> O Lord, I am with thee;
> Thou dost me hold by my right hand,
> And still upholdest me." (Ps. 73.23).

The result of this habitual converse with God in prayer was that in many things relating to God's providence he had much of God's secret. He would warn and comfort his friends with regard to emerging trials or seasons of joy. He would also speak of impending judgements in the wider sphere of world events. There were, perhaps, those who had a greater grasp of theological truth than he, but none in his day enjoyed more of God's presence, or the prophetic insight which comes through God's secret converse with the soul through the written Word. And with him this was sometimes imparted "in the night watches when deep sleep falleth upon men." But since I have elsewhere written a fairly extensive sketch of Norman's life, I need not dwell here on what manner of man he was.

But the Lord had His witnesses among the young as among the old. A little distance from our home in Swainbost were two attractive young sisters who died in their youth. They were both brought under the influence of the Gospel at an early age. If Christina and Marion MacLean were lovely in their life, in death they were lovelier still. During her last illness Christina expressed a desire that members of the family should not sit with her in the night. "When you are here," she would say, "I am alone, but when I am by myself I have the best of company." The presence of the Lord in her soul, and we believe the sensible nearness of God's ministering spirits, transformed her room into a vestible of Heaven. A few moments before she died she seemed to awake out of a deep and prolonged sleep.

She had been unconscious for some time before. Her eyes, momentarily bright with life and joy were looking upward. With her hands stretched upwards and her eyes towards heaven, she cried, in the words of the prophet: "My father, my father, behold the chariot of Israel and the horsemen thereof." (II Kings 2). And, like another when she had said this, she "fell asleep." Before she lost consciousness she had asked that verses from Psalm 84 should be sung before her body was committed to the grave. They were words which proclaimed that while her dust was laid in the earth her soul would be with God, to dwell for evermore in His presence. The words were:

"How lovely is Thy dwelling-place
O Lord of hosts to me,
The tabernacles of Thy grace
How pleasant, Lord, they be."

Her younger sister, Marion, died also in a state of great spiritual comfort. As the curtain between Time and Eternity was being slowly drawn back, she gave expression to her faith and joy in the Lord.

In the quiet world of those early days it was a joy to walk along the village road and listen to the singing of a Psalm which rose up like incense from many homes at evening and morning worship. One should not wish to see the day when in this favoured Isle these accents of piety should no longer be heard from the homes of the people.

We had in our village a home noted for the exquisite quality of its Psalm singing. It was the home of a gracious and elderly lady whom we called "Widow MacLean." One evening two or three lads, including myself, met her near her home. It was a lovely moonlit night. As we stood beside her she began to speak softly about a dear friend who had just died. The memory of her solemn manner, and her wistful upward gaze as she spoke of her friend "singing in glory," still remain a happy picture in my mind. The last days of this worthy lady were largely made up of sighs and smiles. She often sighed that her heavenly Bridegroom was so long in coming. She smiled because He would soon come, as He said, to take her Home. Her excellent grandson, the Rev. Malcolm Morrison, had the privilege of being with her in her last hours. It was a solemn experience to which he often referred.

Although piety shed her golden light over our home we had little of this world's riches. Yet out of her small resources my mother would welcome to her table as many of the Lord's people as she could gather together during sacramental seasons. I can still remember those happy companies and their chaste conversation in Christ. Their talk was invariably on good matter which concerned the King. They would, I remember, tell one another of the way God met them in His Word, and how He would, at times, awake them out of sleep with His Word on their lips. If of earthly substance they had little, those dear people were rich in faith and love and other spiritual blessings.

In those early days my mother would take us aside and warn us of the danger of strong drink. Her earnest exhortations made a deep impression on my mind, and even then I resolved never to enter the drunkard's haunt.

During my first long journey to town, when I was a mere boy, I met a school companion who had money in his pocket. He offered me a shilling so that later on in the day we could have what he called "a drink" together. In those days a shilling was an immense sum of money to a boy, and there were two things I wanted very much to buy. One was "a police whistle" which, I felt, would endow me with a wonderful sense of superiority and power! The other was to get into my hands an enormous piece of the famous ginger bread (aran cridhe) that was sold in great quantities at the annual

Fair outside the town of Stornoway. My generous companion, whom I did not meet that evening, died young. Like so many young men from my native Island, he was led into "the path wherein destroyers go" — the path of alcoholic woe.

There was another day when I met a man in a certain town. I knew him only slightly. He offered me a drink. When I refused his offer he began to tell me in a soft deceptive voice how to initiate myself gradually and harmlessly, into what he called the pleasant habit of drinking. But a louder voice was speaking within my own memory. "Beware, my dear boy, beware!" The voice was that of my mother. And without another word I walked away.

How often have I seen able and naturally kindly young men led by the demon of drink into degradation and misery; and if some of those were, by the grace of God, rescued from the very brink of destruction, others were not . . . .

In those early days there were other incidents which somehow left a deep impression on the mind. These, like framed pictures on the wall of memory, remain with me while many other things are forgotten. I recall, for example, how one evening, with a number of other boys, we were entertaining ourselves by throwing small stones on the corrugated iron roof of a newly erected shed belonging to a somewhat wrathful man in the district. The tiny stones did no damage, but the noise, which was to us a great novelty, annoyed the owner who chased us over the sodden ground. Since I was younger than the others my pace was slower. Once he recognised me he altered his steps and walked towards our home. Whenever he entered the door I also, in a state of great fear, ran towards the house, at the back of which I listened to his loud, angry voice as he told my shocked mother of her wayward boy. As I stood there I trembled at the picture of myself which this man, unwittingly, placed before my eyes. Was this really me? Overwhelmed with shame I would have given a thousand worlds if only I could have vanished out of existence and be no more. But it was a pleasant picture which our neighbour gave me of myself that evening, compared with that awful discovery which God made of my heart in the day He brought me to His mirror, and where, in seeing one whom I could not but recognise as myself,

He said, "Thou art the man." Ever since that hour I have been asking God to look at me, and to let me look on myself, only in His dear Son and in His perfect righteousness.

There was another memorable evening when I was present at a Communion service in Harris, where my father was resident as a lay preacher. It was summer, and the service was in the open air. The day was warm and calm, so that the powerful voice of the preacher — the Rev. R. Macleod, Garrabost — could be heard a long distance away. As the preacher, like Paul of old, "reasoned of righteousness, temperance and judgment to come," a solemn hush rested on the large congregation present. During the sermon the preacher told a story. It was that of a man who sometimes engaged in the dangerous practice of scaling the face of a high precipitous cliff at the base of which snarled the deep and restless sea. This man had a little son who would sometimes steal away to watch his father negotiating the rock. One day, as the father was halfway down, he heard a voice. "Father, I am coming after you." It was the voice of his own son. By his careless example he had led his own child to destruction. The story, of course, was meant as a warning to parents whose example might lead their children astray. From where I sat I could see my Father, and I knew that if I lost my soul it was not because he had not, by precept and example, set before me the way of life and safety.

During those impressionable years there was another incident which somehow has always lodged in my memory. It was that of awakening one lovely summer morning to find that I had slept too long, and had therefore missed a boat on which I intended to sail to another distant isle. I was awakened in good time, but I turned on my side and slept again! I can still recall the feeling of shame and despair which touched my mind as I stood, too late, on the shore to watch the boat far out at sea, and I left behind. The incident, trivial in itself, was to me at that moment deeply symbolic. I had slept in! I was left behind! I was too late! What if in the hour of death I should awake to discover that, spiritually, I had slept throughout the brief day of grace and that the door of Heaven was finally shut? What if in an eternity of remorse I should remember my awful folly and neglect? Even now as I think of that moment I feel concern lest, by relaxing in the race set before me, I should lose Christ and the joys which are reserved at God's Right Hand for as many as shall endure to the end.

During the summer school vacation we lived a carefree pastoral life. In the morning I would lead forth a number of the village cattle toward a lovely fringe of green pasture land which lay by the shore. There I would spend the day with only the sun to tell me the time, and the brook, the sea and the sand to provide me with pastime.

This fringe of shore is associated in my memory with a young girl from our village. Her name was Annie MacRitchie. The cloudless summer day was already drawing to a close when she appeared all alone at the end of the path leading down to the shore. Her step was slow, for an incurable consumption had already weakened her body. She was dressed in white, and had come to take a look at the scenes of her childhood days. But she stood among us, calm and happy. Then she walked away, her graceful figure in perfect harmony with the deep beauty of that place, the flowers of which seemed to smile all day. Although we children did not know it, in that girl's soul there was an undying love to Christ.

This found expression in the words of the Psalm:

"God is of mine inheritance
And cup the portion;
The lot that fallen is to me
Thou dost maintain alone.

"Unto me happily the lines
In pleasant places fell:
Yea the inheritance I got
In beauty doth excel." (Ps. 16).

I can never think of that vanished figure in white without associating her with the redeemed multitude who stand before God's Throne in the garments of life and immortality.

But the carefree days of my own boyhood years were coming to an end. The days of bodily pain and deep spiritual concern had arrived.

CHAPTER THREE

A NIGHT TO BE REMEMBERED

I was still very young when a virulent infection invaded one of my knees. One morning after losing consciousness, a pious neighbour prayed that God would graciously receive my departing spirit. Death passed me by, however, and after a period of about two years I could walk again with ease.

After I recovered from this illness, I had moments of seriousness when I secretly turned to the Bible and kneeled in prayer. I recall how, on a lovely summer evening as the rays of the western sun were streaming through our windows at Swainbost, I sat alone in the house reading the Bible. I remember being much affected by the rich and vivid symbolism of the Book of Revelation. The glories of the heavenly world seemed to open up to my young imagination, The varied and transcendent beauties of that world, and the happiness of all who dwell there, solemnised and melted my heart. But that moment of joy coincided with the birth of a great sorrow, for it was also the moment when a dark and evil thought invaded my mind. I felt like one struck down by a blow from an unseen and cruel hand. The world appeared to darken; and a cloud of fear settled on my mind. Such a thought, I concluded, seldom entered the mind of any other man. That evening marked the beginning of a misery which continued with me for many years. Whether the unwelcome thought arose out of my own sinful mind, or was put there by some evil spirit, made no difference to me. The thought was mine, and I must be answerable to God for it at last. I also saw that the heart out of which it came was, indeed, "desperately wicked." Thus, so early in life I had to lie in a spiritual prison house without a star in my sky. This secret sorrow I locked in my own bosom.

If I had poured my complaint into an understanding and sympathetic ear, I might possibly have been relieved. But this I was both ashamed and afraid to do. To pretend that my heart was merry I took part in vain amusements. God, however, preserved me from gross outward sins.

Shortly afterwards my father left Lewis for the lovely Isle of Berneray in Harris, where he laboured as lay missionary for about nine years. When I reached the age of eighteen years, I, with other local lads, was called to the army, for the Great War was then raging in Europe. Meantime, however, we decided that instead of army service, we should go to sea. Supplied by local fishermen with over-generous proofs of our maritime qualifications we left for Stornoway. The examining doctor received all the lads kindly, except me, whom he rejected on account of the sensitive scar below my knee. Shortly afterwards, in October 1918, my companions left for a Southern seaport and I became a soldier. I came home before the end of the year.

On a grey and stormy New Year's morning in 1919 we were shocked to hear that two of my companions with many other sailors, all happy to be home, perished off the coast of Lewis. As I stood before the open grave of one of my companions whose body was found, and with the light of the moon showing the outline of a coffin, I wondered what strange providence had divided our ways.

After my return from the army, I was engaged as an apprentice shipwright in the town of Greenock. There, for a time, I was fairly comfortable in my mind, apart from frequent seasons of anxiety which the recollection of my particular and terrifying sinful thoughts brought me. But soon my concern and anxiety began to deepen. The attempt to get away from my sorrow by singing and dancing at local Highland gatherings only aggravated my sore, and made the burden more intolerable. My fear of being carried away to a lost eternity became so acute that I was afraid my very face reflected the awful sense of guilt which oppressed my mind.

During this time of extreme spiritual concern it never occurred to me to discontinue attending the means of Grace. I was also unwilling to give up the prayer which my father put in my mouth as a child. It was about the only thing I could cling to in that violent storm which now shook my whole being. This inconsistency of mixing foolish frivolity with attendance at Church services did not escape the notice of some who, unknown to me, were interested in my spiritual welfare.

One evening a young domestic servant spoke very earnestly and tenderly to me about my conduct. She ended her remarks by saying that God would show me mercy if I sought Him with all my heart. In the presence of that beautiful Christian girl I felt that her eyes looked straight into my soul. As I turned away from her I had a strong conviction that her "word in season" was from God. The question I now kept asking myself was — "Can it be that there is really hope for ME, and that God can forgive MY sin?" At that time I passed through an emotional experience which, I suppose, helped to relieve the inward tension from which I had suffered so long.

I now discontinued my attendance at the Saturday night Gaelic concerts and dances. My conscience severely rebuked me each time I entered the haunts of so-called "pleasure."

One Sabbath morning shortly afterwards, as I sat in Church, I was surprised to see a tall minister walking through the vestry door and sitting down in the precentor's box below the pulpit. Then I heard hurried footsteps walking down the aisle, and presently a hand was placed on my shoulder and a compelling voice said, "Come, my lad, come at once." I looked round to see the anxious face of old Alexander Mackay, the elder, whom I followed to the door. As we moved round to the side of the Church and passed through two doors, I was terrified to find myself facing the congregation. Mr Mackay then addressed the occupant of the box, asking him to ascend to the pulpit, and saying that I would lead the praise. The service was in Gaelic. A mist came over my eyes and my knees began to tremble. Only that I knew the Psalm by heart and that "St David" was one of my "foolproof" tunes, I would have failed in my task. But that morning marked the beginning of my deep affection for the unknown stranger who occupied the pulpit. He was the Rev. Andrew Sutherland of Duke Street Free Church, in Glasgow, who afterwards became my life-long friend.

It was about this time that along with a companion, I attended a Fellowship meeting in the local Free Presbyterian congregation. The "Question" was based on the words: "For ye were sometime darkness, but now are ye light in the Lord, walk as children of light." The minister, the Rev. E. MacQueen, ended the service with words which seemed to drench the minds and melt the hearts of many present. How I envied the people of God, and how I prayed at that moment that I might be like them. The Word was with power. The preacher dwelt tenderly on the love of Christ to sinners. One of his stories I still remember. It was about a worthy Catechist in the north who found his servant girl one day in the field praying. Her face was wet with tears. The good man remarked on how envious he was of her tears, while he himself was afflicted with a hard heart that left his eyes dry. She replied: "Oh! Mr Munro, if you had an entrance into the love of Christ, you would know of something which no heart, however hard, would withstand." Throughout the service I had a strong conviction that I was among a people, many of whom had entered a world and who enjoyed something to which I was a stranger. There was an air of reality and peace about the service. That evening I listened — as I had done sometimes before — to the wonderful story of God's love for the souls of men, and of His coming down in the Person of His own Son into our fallen world to redeem us and reconcile us by His Blood. I heard of the free and open pathway between the soul and God through Christ, and of the indwelling of the Holy Spirit to quicken us and to prepare us for Heaven.

As I listened I silently asked God to bless me also. Earnestly I prayed in my heart that I might know the great and wonderful salvation which the message proclaimed.

It was then that something happened. It was as if Someone had opened the long shut door of my heart and just walked in. My whole inward being was, as it were, invaded by a power which was both sweet and life-giving. It was a new thing which had never touched my spirit before. My consciousness was flooded by something like a gentle warm wave of light, life and love. God, I felt, had in mercy, broken through the awful barrier of my sin, and had saved me from its dominion, guilt and power. He had, for Christ's sake, forgiven all my sins and cast them into the depths of the sea. He had forgiven and forgotten, but how much He forgave I may never know. In His grace and kindness He brought me also into a new world and had, as I hoped, changed me into a "new creation". My soul, like a restless dove, had now found its place of rest in the clefts of the Rock of Ages.

That evening I felt especially as if I had been lifted out of a cold, dark grave by a gentle—if unseen—hand. The shadow of death under which I so long pined seemed to give way before the sweet consoling light communicated to my soul by the Spirit of God. As the preacher enlarged on his theme I knew that a miracle of a resurrection was taking place in my spiritual life. The Lord passed by me and said—"Live." The precious blood of the covenant seemed to drop on my conscience, giving peace where a sense of guilt had through the years oppressed me almost to despair. I also saw with the inner eye how God was just in justifying the ungodly who believe in Jesus. The poor and stricken lad who had entered God's House without hope, because he was without Christ, could now rejoice in both. As I remember it, a Psalm was also sung at the close of the service which truly expressed God's love and mercy in saving a poor sinner like me. The words were:

"He from His sanctuary's height
Hath downward cast His eye;
And from His glorious throne in Heaven
The Lord the earth did spy.

That of the mournful prisoner
The groanings He might hear,
To set them free that unto death
By men appointed were." (Ps. 102).

Outside the hall I was but dimly conscious of the presence of men. I remember, however, how the mantle of gloom which, for me, had rested on all creation was now removed, and all things seemed to smile, as it were, at this great wonder — a sinner reconciled to God. This, I hope, was a night to be forever remembered, in which the Lord made a pathway through the deep for me to an unfading inheritance.

There were friends at the service who, somehow, knew that my bonds were loosed. One of them was Mary Murray, North Tolsta, who had spoken to me so earnestly a few days before. They led me away to their place of residence where we were very happy. But I was like one who dreamed. My sackcloth had fallen off me and I was given the garment of praise. The thought of my sin being forgiven and put away filled me with a sense of unbelievable wonder.

The deep joy which possessed my soul that night was truly unspeakable. I had tasted of the poor, superficial pleasures of this world, but what had entered my soul that evening made, by comparison, the most desirable earthly joys taste sour, insipid and unwanted. This was, I knew, the true God and life eternal. I had found the Tree of Life, and with King Solomon, after his painful quest for happiness, I could say — "I sat under His shadow with great delight." I had found the Heavenly Treasure and the Living Well. The joy of having found Christ, the Pearl of great price, I could not describe. The God Whom I had so often looked upon as terrible in His wrath had now, I hoped, embraced me in the arms of His love and mercy. Those everlasting arms would, I knew, from that hour, uphold me in every trial that might overtake me in this life. To have missed this unspeakable gift would be to suffer eternal despair, loneliness and destitution. In that hour, I realised that those who let God's gift of eternal life, offered to them in Christ, pass by unsought and ignored, must spend endless ages weeping over their folly and awful loss.

When, in after days, I studied my Bible and read Christian biography I found that the experience of that evening was not a unique or isolated thing. It was not an emotional release or any upsurge of mere feeling. It was not a passing phase of mental exaltation. It was something which multitudes of God's people had known and enjoyed in every age. It is the soul in intimate communion with a Person, Who — why we just cannot tell — wants to communicate Himself and His love to us forever and ever. He gave Himself for us that He might give Himself to us. He loved men, not for what they are, but in spite of what they are. The wonder of this shall continue to deepen throughout eternal ages. And

He shall never cease to love those who trust in Him. The universe has no wonder to compare with this.

Long afterwards I read books by such men as Augustine, Pascal, John Calvin, Thomas Goodwin, Thomas Chalmers, C. H. Spurgeon, John Kennedy and many others. The lives and works of such men prove, if proof is required, that the Christian life with its hope and enjoyments, belongs to a dimension which lies nearer to Ultimate Reality than any other. Spiritual love, peace, joy, with the consciousness of God's presence in our lives, are aspects of Reality deeper and more solid than anything belonging to the world of mere nature.

I also came to know that we enter this glorious spiritual world in exactly the same way as our bodies enter this lower world. Before we enter it we must, in the words of our Lord, be "born again." It would, for example, be impossible for us to know anything of this natural world — in fact we would have no existence at all — unless we entered it through the miracle of birth. The loveliness of the dawn and of the star-lit sky we could never otherwise behold. In the same way, we cannot enter the spiritual world, or have any apprehension of its glory, apart from the greater miracle of a spiritual rebirth. The Bible, therefore, says: "Eye hath not seen, ear hath not heard, neither hath it entered into the heart of man what God hath prepared for them who love Him." This miracle of enlightenment takes place the moment we embrace Christ as our personal Redeemer and yield to His holy Will and claims as these are revealed in the Bible. Although we are as yet on the fringe of this world, we know that its blessings will forever enrich and gladden our souls. In God's presence there is fulness of joy. At His right hand there are pleasures for ever more.

But I soon learned that my life here was not to be perpetual calm or sunshine. Nature, for the growth, maturity and perfection of her flowers and plants, with their varied beauties and colours, keeps a wonderful balance. There is night and day. There is summer and winter. There is sunshine and cloud. So it is in the higher realm of God's grace. The work of progressive holiness in the soul, by which God prepares us for Heaven, often means trial, discipline and pain. "As many as I love, I rebuke and chasten."

Often since that wonderful evening I had to endure pain and suffering. But He who knows our frame is with His own in every crisis and in every valley of darkness, grief and fear. Whatever may happen, either in the world or in our personal circumstances, in His hands we are supremely and everlastingly safe. He shall make all things to work together for our good. This is the promise of the Lord to all who commit their soul into His hand as into the hand of a faithful Creator.

Within a year of my conversion I remembered the Lord's death in the ordinance of the Supper. At a preparatory service, Dr Alexander Stewart, of Edinburgh, preached a comforting sermon on the words — "My grace is sufficient for thee." Afterwards I applied for permission to sit at the Lord's Table. The following Sabbath I listened to a memorable sermon from the words: "I am He that liveth and was dead." The theme was Christ's sufferings and the glory which followed. That day I wept much as I heard of the love that Christ had for sinners in dying for them. Going home, I retired to my bedroom. There, in much peace, I covenanted with the Lord to be His forever.

In those days even my sleep was sweet to me. Whether this was the result of the blessing I enjoyed I cannot tell, but some of those dreams which I then had were to me very solemn. In fact they are at this moment as vivid to my mind as they were when they first appeared out of that unknown land where such dreams are born. I recall, for instance, how on three successive nights I dreamt of the Lord Jesus. In the last of these I dreamt I saw myself walking alone toward the green meadow near the Swainbost shore where, as I mentioned before, I used to play as a boy. In the middle of this quiet hollow I could see a number of people who seemed to be very, very happy. In this group stood a Person whom I knew to be the Lord. I also knew some of the people present — all of whom have since, I believe, gone to their rest in Heaven. As I walked wonderingly toward this happy company the One on whom all eyes rested came forward to meet me. He welcomed me into the company and most tenderly spoke to me, but what he said I may not tell. It was truly a word in season and a cherished word of love. This was

only a dream. It might have been that the Lord thus accommodated Himself to my state of spiritual childhood, or it might have been due to the fact that at the time of my 'first love' Christ was never absent from my thoughts. I never had a dream since in which I saw the Lord Jesus. "The just shall live by faith" in the invisible God, and in that "more sure word of prophecy; whereunto ye do well that ye take heed, as unto a light that shineth in a dark place, until the day dawn, and the day star arise in your hearts." (2 Pet. 1.). If one were to leave the solid rock of Scripture for such night visions one would be very unwise. Whatever place dreams may now have in the Christian life — and here I do record some of mine — God's sure communication of His mind to His people is always by means of the written infallible and inspired Word. On that Word alone — and on Christ the Word Incarnate — my faith wholly rests as the only true and everlasting foundation.

CHAPTER FOUR

COLLEGE DAYS

IN GREENOCK I lodged for a season with a Mr John MacKenzie, a native of Campbeltown in Argyll. John was blessed with a good wife who set an excellent example before us all. In those days John was destitute of all spiritual seriousness or concern. To his other sins he added one of resentment against some of the teachings of Scripture, and would sometimes speak of the "contradictions" which could be found in the Bible. The day came, however, when God brought him to seek mercy and forgiveness at the Throne of Grace, and when he could rejoice in God's Salvation. God's statutes then became his songs, and God's Word he accepted as the perfect revelation of His Will and Grace. "How is it," he was once asked, "that you now believe what you formerly denied?" "In those days," said John, "I was ignorant of the Author of Scripture, but now that I know Him, I know also that every Word of God is true," Mr MacKenzie afterwards became an elder in our local Church.

In 1923 I was received as a student of the Free Church of Scotland. If the prospect of preaching the Gospel filled me with much concern, it also filled me with immeasurable joy. And so one early morning I put away my carpenter's tools and left for Edinburgh. The kindly Rev. A. M. Renwick, who was then minister at Dumbarton, and convener of our Admissions Committee, I found most helpful and understanding.

From the din of the shipyard I immediately moved into the quieter and more dignified atmosphere of a theological hall. There, even in the earlier stages of my studies, I was privileged to dine with a very learned and godly company of men. Though a student of a small church, I knew that around that table, with its simple fare, there sat some of the excellent of the earth. In that 'large upper room,' which overlooked the whole of Princes Street, we were a happy band. The learned and godly Professor J. R. MacKay was the man who commanded most attention. A massive man physically, he had a voice of peculiar earnestness and power. When in his preaching he warmed to some great and congenial theme like "the Everlasting Covenant," "The Priesthood of Christ," or "Imputed Righteousness," his words and voice touched one in an unusual way. He was a man who appeared to dwell on the higher theological altitudes.

Professor R. Moore, who was an Irishman, had the wit of his race. His prayers were remarkable for their freshness and depth, and they could often touch one's heart. He was, however, one of those men who could absorb knowledge easily without any considerable ability to give out what he had formerly taken in.

The humane and affectionate Professor J. K. Cameron could never — even amid his trials — get rid of a smile which he carried with him like a perpetual benediction, while his like-minded colleague, Professor D. MacLean, would sometimes delight us by preaching choice and deeply impressive sermons charged with evangelical warmth.

In less than two years I was deemed fit to enter the University as a regular student in Arts. I regret to say that the three years I spent at the University had a very withering effect on my spiritual life. Unwittingly, I wandered into a dead and dreary region. My devotional life ebbed till I could find nothing in myself but a cold, listless heart which, for a season, often remained unaffected by the Truth, and unmoved by my prayers.

In Edinburgh I became a member of St Columba Free Church, of which Dr Alexander Stewart was the minister. Dr Stewart was an arresting preacher whose pleasant voice and literary appreciations could not fail to command attention. His English was precise, without being prosaic, while the rich theological and experimental content of his sermons could be most edifying. It was in his native Gaelic, however, that he 'let himself go'. The tension of speaking to professors, students, and other intellectual varieties, he then abandoned. In his Gaelic preaching he was the perfect master of the Highland **"seis,"** (or, in Welsh, "hwyl"), which so many Highland ministers inherited, from men like Dr John MacDonald of Ferintosh. The great advantage of the **"seis"** in the old days was that by its judicious use a hard, strong voice could be rendered pleasing and often very affecting. A musical ear was necessary for its use. In the large open-air gatherings of other days this pleasant enunciation of the Gospel message was never considered an affectation, but as something irresistible and spontaneous, and which also added dignity and unction to the preacher's theme.

Principal MacLeod's appreciation of Dr Alexander Stewart as a preacher could be voiced by all who had listened to that earnest herald of the Evangel. One of Dr Stewart's sermons stands out in my memory with unfading clarity. It was on the Bride's joyous recognition of the Bridegroom's voice in the Song. "The voice of my Beloved, behold he cometh . . ." The call of that voice was ever toward greater discoveries and realisations of His power, grace and love. It was a voice she had heard in her effectual calling out of death and darkness into a new state of life and communion with her Lord. She had heard it also calling her away from the things which would have diverted her eyes and heart from Himself. And with her pilgrimage here over, she had heard it calling her into the mansions of Glory. She would hear it again on the last day when, in her resurrection, He would quicken and glorify her precious dust.

A life-long friend of Dr Stewart was the Rev. George MacKay of Fearn, who sometimes preached in Edinburgh in those days. This greatly beloved man I came to know well. His much-blessed ministry in the island of Lewis was the happiest time in his life, and his allusions to that "blessed island" were an indication of how deep was his affection for a people who loved him as God's ambassador. Mr MacKay studied his sermons with great care. Every word and thought were given their due place and emphasis in his message. His voice was far-reaching and extremely well managed. But to his audience his sermons sounded fresh, as if each thought emerged there and then from the hidden springs of Truth. At a communion in Glasgow, for example, he once paced the floor in our home for a whole afternoon carefully preparing the sermon which he was to preach that evening. It was based on a passage of Scripture which contains the words — "Fear not . . . . I am Alpha and Omega, the beginning and the end, the First and the Last." In the midst of his perambulations he asked me what was the proper Gaelic word for "bier". That evening he preached a wonderful sermon. Among many other impressive things he said, "This was He who stood by the cradle of the universe when it was born, and who shall stand by its bier when it shall finally pass away."

During my student days I once heard Mr MacKay in Lochaber. His theme on that occasion was the Syrophoenician woman who perservered in her prayers till the Lord answered her plea. He went on to speak of her new-born joy at the prospect of sitting forever at her Lord's feet to enjoy the sweet crumbs which would fall from His table to nourish her soul. The sustained and vivid way in which he dwelt on the response of the soul to the loving kindness of the Lord, delivering his sermon in the traditional **"seis,"** is now almost as clear in my memory as when he stood before us in that little church in Fort William. Mr MacKay was a messenger whose feet were, in his day, truly beautiful on the Gospel mountain.

A well-known contemporary of Mr MacKay was the Rev. Roderick MacLeod of Garrabost, whose name I have already mentioned. I listened to Mr MacLeod several times during my College days. To oratorical gifts and a strong voice he added, in his younger days, a large measure of self-confidence. But God taught him the needed lesson of which he was not ashamed to tell. Once he was present at a communion. On the Sabbath morning he listened to a colleague whose gifts of utterance could not compare with his own. During the sermon he began to whisper to himself about the quality of the sermon; but saying that when he would stand there in the evening, the people would hear something to remember. But in the evening, as he stood up to preach, he suddenly found himself in the distressing toils of mental and vocal bondage. Both his mind and tongue refused to function. He could only repeat the text, and add to it a few halting words. He went down the pulpit stair that night deeply embarrassed. God, however, had blessed His own Word in the experience of at least one present. That evening he learned the lesson that God does not always bless man's "excellency of speech," but His own Word — even on the lips of the poorest of men.

If some of the sermons I listened to in those days still linger in the memory, so do some public prayers; and here I may refer to one of the most solemn and spiritual prayers I ever heard in this world. It was by the Rev. Norman Matheson of Kilmorack, in our church in Glenmoriston. The sermon which followed was, by comparison, commonplace. It seemed to me that the sermon was, more or less, his own, while his prayer was breathed through his soul by the Spirit of God.

In the year 1928 the Church sent me to Fort William, Ontario, for the summer vacation. The colony of Gaelic-speaking Highlanders who had settled down in that town had services in their own tongue. A kinder people never lived, and to me my visit among them was a happy season.

A few Sabbaths after my arrival in Canada, a young and very intelligent married woman came to one of our services. Almost immediately she was struck down in deep conviction of sin. That morning, as I remember the story, she had been up early to prepare for a "Sunday outing." But meantime something happened. The soft distant melody of a Gaelic Psalm, such as she was accustomed to hear sung by a large congregation in her native Lewis, seemed to captivate her inner ear. The Psalm and its music were very real to her. So much so that instead of profaning the Sabbath she decided to go to church. That day she became a seeker of the City that has foundations. Her gracious and consistent afterlife proved that the arrow which smote her heart that morning was from the King's bow. That week I tasted of a new joy, the joy of being the means of bringing a soul to the Lord.

One afternoon in Fort William I visited an elderly Christian woman. When I appeared at the door she remarked with evident surprise; "How wonderful that you should be here at this moment! I had just been dreaming that you were here with me, and that together we sang the words:

> For mercy shall be built, said I,
> Forever to endure;
> Thy faithfulness, e'en in the heav'ns
> Thou wilt establish sure." (Ps. 89 v. 2).

"In that case," I said, — as I remember this incident — "let the dream become a reality. Let us sing it together now." This we did, and the memory of that sweet moment with the Lord 'in the midst,' lingers on.

At the weekly Prayer Meeting on another evening I offered some remarks on the words: "If I may but touch His clothes I shall be whole." The good men who engaged in prayer seemed to enjoy spiritual freedom and nearness to the Lord. Some time afterwards I visited a woman of whose affliction and its cure I was unaware. The victim of a trying skin disease, she was brought into a state of physical and nervous exhaustion. At the meeting that night, as the Word of God began to affect her mind and heart, she felt a curious sensation pass over the surface of her body. There and then her trouble vanished. I was amazed at this instance of how the Word, when believed, can sometimes, and when the Lord wills, bring health to the body as well as to the soul. But I am no believer in the cult of "faith-healing" carried on through other means and in other ways.

It was in Fort William that I was privileged with a long and intimate contact with one of the greatest men of his generation. I refer to Principal John MacLeod. For about two weeks he and his gracious wife lodged with the same lady with whom I stayed. They were doing the "trans-continental" journey from Australia, and being in indifferent health at the time he made the journey home leisurely. My first contact, however, with Dr MacLeod had been on his own native heath in Lochaber a few years before. I had been sent there for the summer vacation to preach in the local church. As the communion Sabbath was observed during that period, he arrived on the scene and conducted all the services. The congregation was small, but that made no difference to the excellent quality of his message. His lips poured out a warm stream of evangelic truth, during which he touched on all the great themes of the Gospel. A sermon which he preached in the village of Treslaig, on the bank of Loch Lhinne, was characteristic. "We have Abraham as our father," was his subject. It was meant as a reminder to those in the audience who could boast of godly ancestors that grace and godliness did not come by a natural descent. Two other sermons of his on "The sinner reasoning with

God," and "God's Book of Remembrance," will, always, remain a much valued recollection.

When I, therefore, met him in Canada we were no strangers, although as a mere youth I could not but feel somewhat shy in the presence of such a great man, At table he could entertain and edify the company with stories of past worthies in the Highlands, some of which I afterwards wrote down. This invaluable information, I knew, would never again come my way. His phenomenal memory reflected itself in the way in which he could give the life history of quite obscure, if godly, men and women. And he could see the humour which so often enters into the human situation. He was a finished scholar of great depth; and when he touched on higher matters, whether in the realm of history, theology or languages, one felt in the presence of a mind to which knowledge came with great ease. He carried the scholar's mantle without ostentation. Had his ambition kept pace with his abilities, he would have had no compeer in his generation. Free from all the petty ambitions which vex smaller minds, he was quite indifferent to the honour which comes from man. The fact that he began his ministry in a small Free Presbyterian congregation in a remote West Highland village, proved that his affinities and affections were ever with the afflicted people of God.

In the Isle of Skye, I once shared Communion services with Principal MacLeod. Before I entered the pulpit, and in a very affectionate voice, he mentioned how an elderly minister in Lochaber once said to him that in preaching the Gospel he should always remember that he was God's ambassador, and that his words and spirit should show Whose he was and Whom he served. This was a word of exhortation which, I hope, I sought to follow in after days.

Before his last illness I saw him at a meeting of the Commission of Assembly in Edinburgh. A member was on the floor delivering a long and high sounding speech. The Principal appeared to be taking notes, or preparing a speech of his own. When the speaker sat down he handed me a used envelope on the back of which was an excellent translation into Gaelic of the famous hymn: "There is a fountain filled with blood . . . ." This precious fragment I kept over the years.

When, before my ordination, I appeared before the Presbytery of Inverness it was he who examined me in Greek. The two questions which he put to me on that occasion were so phrased that I had only to answer "Yes" or "No". "You would not say ———?" "But you would say ———?" He then turned to the Moderator and expressed his full satisfaction with my answers. For a man who knew his subject better than any other in his generation, his graciousness and sympathy I could never forget.

Shortly before he died I went to see him. With much feeling he greeted me in the words: "Hitherto ye have asked nothing in My Name; ask and ye shall receive, that your joy may be full." In these words he found honey, some of which he would have shared with others. When in 1948 he was taken Home many felt that a great light had been removed from the earth.

During my College days I stayed for a season at Fort Augustus with a Mrs MacNaughton, a native of Inverness. This gifted and Godly woman was the grand-daughter of an excellent layman,—I think, John MacDonald by name—who lived at Leys, near Inverness. John was a bright witness in his day. She once told me of an experience which befell her on the day he died. She was on a path leading to his home when her mind and ears were arrested by songs of exquisite sweetness and melody. Never before did she hear anything remotely resembling the heavenly songs which filled the sky at the moment when the soul of her aged relative was taken home to God.

One day as I was looking over some of her books I came across a New Testament which had been riddled with bullet holes. It bore the name of her son who had been killed in the Great World War. He was, I believe, the subject of her continual prayers. When later I touched on this sad memory she told me of a dream she had on the night of his death. In her dream she found herself in France where, in an open field, she saw many Highland soldiers stretched out on the ground — some wounded and some dead. Among the dead she found her own boy. This was more than a dream for, as she was afterwards informed, he was killed at that very hour. Afterwards when a picture of his grave reached her she recognised the place where, in her dream, she had knelt over the lifeless body of her son. But who can understand these mysteries of the human spirit, or the deep instinctive bond between a mother and her child?

Another memory of my student days is that of staying for a week-end in Dumfries with a lady who sat for some years under the preaching of C. H. Spurgeon, the renowned Baptist preacher. Before we retired to rest she read a page from his devotional "Evening Readings." The hushed affectionate manner in which she mentioned his name made me realise the enduring place which that great herald of God had in the love and esteem of the multitudes who came within the sound of his voice.

More impressive, perhaps, was a brief contact I once made with an old hearer of Doctor Kennedy, who lived outside Tain. This lady was elderly, bedridden and, I think, alone. In answer to a question as to her welfare she made no mention of her bodily enfeeblement or temporal straits. "You ask me," she replied, "how I am. As the Godly Doctor would say — 'There are seasons when clouds take Him out of my sight'." From this remark I gathered that God's gracious Presence was her one consolation on earth, while the absence of it was her source of sorrow. It was the dove-like and authentic voice of one who had lived in the days of Gospel power in the north. This excellent woman, Jean Munro by name, died in 1930.

During my college vacations I occasionally accompanied my father to the Summer communions in Uist and Harris. These were happy seasons during which one could make contact with many choice Christians. Once at Leverburgh I was led into the company of a young man whose Christian disposition and conversation impressed me deeply. On a Sabbath evening I accompanied this young man along the willowed road to Rodel. It was truly an Emmaus walk; for as this young man opened his heart and began to relate what God had done for his soul, a deep peace took possession of our spirits. We both felt that Another was with us. I never saw my friend again. He died soon afterwards.

In Harris I made the acquaintance of an excellent Christian man known as Malcolm (or "Calum") MacLeod. Malcolm was a man who enjoyed much of God's secret. Between him and my father there was a tender bond of Christian affection. While in Berneray my father once engaged a boat to collect peats in a distant isle. It was a calm, deceptive day in winter. Returning home, the heavily-loaded boat had to battle against a contrary wind and a rising storm. Darkness fell, and the heavy seas began to pass over our heads. The man in charge could not control the storm-swept boat, while we were all stricken with fear. Mercifully the sail was pulled down, and we drifted on in the darkness. At last we were tossed behind a small island where we sheltered for some time. He whose pathway is in the sea preserved us in those raging billows.

That afternoon one of Malcolm's sons — the late Rev. Lachlan MacLeod — climbed a hill near his native village of Borve and, with his glass, he tried to locate us out at sea. In the unsettled twilight he saw us battling with the storm, but with a fresh outbreak of the blizzard, and in the gathering darkness he thought he saw us disappearing in an angry splash of broken waves. Returning home he told his father the sad news of our loss. Malcolm at once sought counsel in prayer from Him Who sits as King on the flood. Returning from the "secret place" he made straight for our home where he informed my anxious mother that before a certain hour that night she would welcome us at the door. A few minutes before the hour he mentioned we arrived at our home. I have often thought since then that our preservation from a watery grave was, under the good hand of the Lord, due to the prayers of this holy man.

A few years before he died Malcolm had a remarkable dream, an account of which afterwards appeared in several Church magazines. In his dream he found himself standing on a lovely green slope on which lay robes of great beauty. On the front of each robe were inscribed the words — "Repentance," "Regeneration" and "Holiness," while on the back of each the words — "Eternal Holiness" were written in clear and shining letters. In a way that he could not understand he found himself clothed in one of these, and his joy and comfort were indescribable. Presently, however, he was grieved to see a black, rusty object moving out of his breast which, miraculously, did no damage to the garment in which he was arrayed. An unknown person who stood near him explained that this painful crook was his own sin, and that when the work of grace was perfected in his soul he would be brought into a state of "Eternal Holiness." Malcolm believed that his dream was of God.

The day this worthy man died my father had a strong premonition that he would soon be separated from his friend. Hurrying towards his home he found him dying, while his beloved daughter stood weeping at the door. He was still conscious, and very, very happy. After a fond farewell he lifted up his hand and pronounced the apostolic benediction: "The grace of our Lord Jesus Christ, and the love of God, and the communion of the Holy Ghost be with us all . . ." Having done this he passed into the presence of the Lord. To another friend who asked him how he felt as he was now passing through the last river, he replied that he was going through it, but that since the Lord was with him he had no fear or awareness of the fact.

I finished my course in college, happy that though the Church I wished to serve was small, it like other smaller denominations had remained faithful to the eternal verities of the Gospel. A Church is big, not in its geographical dimensions or numerical strength, but in the measure of its faithfulness to God's Word. When a neighbour teased the famous philosopher, Immanuel Kant, about the diminished size of his garden he replied: "Yes, but think of it **upwards**." It is loyalty to the heavenly Revelation enshrined in the Bible that lends nobility and greatness to a Church. If we lack this, whatever our claims and pretensions, we shrink to the size and poverty of mere earthly things.

Chapter Five

GLENMORISTON

In August 1930, I was, in ecclesiastical phrase, licensed to preach the Gospel. Though called to become the pastor of easier congregations, I was led to consider the needs of Fort Augustus and Glenmoriston, which in those days had quite a considerable bi-lingual congregation.

The day of my ordination was calm and beautiful beyond any day I can remember. The purple hills which rise by the banks of Loch Ness had their perfect and undisturbed reflection in its waters, while the clearer waters of the Caledonian Canal seemed to mirror even quieter skies and greener trees. I recall how I could bless God that my sense of inward peace was in keeping with the serene world around me.

There was present at the service that day one of the most attractive Christians of his generation. He was one of my Glenmoriston elders. His name was Hugh Mackenzie. A man of prayer and deep piety, his very face at times seemed to shine with the light of Heaven. Hugh was like a man who had 'found great spoil.' His happiness was derived from his almost constant communion with God. Principal John MacLeod used to speak of a cluster of Christian men in the North who were remarkable in their day. They had several things in common. They were humble; they were happy; they were childlike and transparent; and they were free from the habitual censoriousness which so often marks and mars the lives of less spiritual men. Hugh, though almost illiterate, was the Principal's friend, and to observe his joyous reactions to his stories in the Manse of Glenmoriston enabled one to see that only a Christian can be a truly happy man.

At that time Hugh was head gamekeeper on the Ceannacroc Estate. One year the estate was leased to a young Indian prince. The wealthy maharajah arrived by special train at Fort Augustus. With him was a retinue of friends and attendants. His sway over his our kindred was kind but absolute. On the Sabbath morning after his arrival, and when Hugh was preparing to leave for church, a subordinate arrived at his door requesting him to have everything ready for the hill at a certain hour. "You tell his highness," said Hugh, "that today I serve another Prince," The man was astonished at the unheard of refusal. The outing was at once cancelled and the courteous oriental prince apologised to Hugh later for, unconsciously, embarrassing him in his religious convictions on the previous day. The Christian bearing and Christlike spirit of a Highland gamekeeper made a deep impression on the maharajah. He pleaded with him to visit India with Mrs Mackenzie as his personal guests. But Hugh refused the generous offer; for he was happy and contented in his own beloved Glenmoriston. Who knows but that a heathen mind in contact with a true man of God may have seen the great difference between his own "religion of despair" and the Gospel of salvation and hope?

There was a minister in the North who used to tell of a service he once conducted in the Great Glen. During the first prayer he was sensible of a hard spiritual atmosphere which, however, presently changed, giving a deeply comforting sense of God's presence. Someone, he felt, had arrived at the service and had brought a blessing with him. When he opened his eyes, Hugh Mackenzie was standing near with a prayer on his lips — as he was wont — and his very face expressive of "the joy of the Lord."

There were other members of our Kirk Session, such as Mr R. Dean, Mr "Sandy" MacDonald, Mr Alex Fraser, who were among the excellent of the earth. Mr Donald MacPherson, Glenurquhart, was these men's friend in the Lord. Donald's mind was exact and expansive. His Christian experience was also deep and real. He was a man who, spiritually speaking, had done business in great waters. His spiritual conflicts often brought him to the Throne of Grace for the needed strength. In our Manse at Fort Augustus his earnest but subdued voice could be heard in the night as he wrestled with the Lord in prayer.

Donald once prayed at family worship in a home where a student of Divinity belonging to one of the larger denominations was present. He enjoyed much freedom. He was brought into that state of mind where Time, because it touched Eternity, seemed to be at a standstill. The amazed student said afterwards that his period at College did not provide him with such genuine spiritual light as reached his mind through that one prayer by an uneducated Highland elder.

My beloved friend Hugh I saw on his death-bed. His joy at the prospect of seeing the Lamb on Mount Zion remained with him to the end. The truly appropriate words, "Blessed are the meek," are engraven on the stone which marks the grave where his dust rests by a willowed brook in upper Glenmoriston.

Among the elect ladies who graced our services in those days in Glenmoriston was Mrs Fullerton who lived at the Inver, and who, in her old age, would have her devoted daughters wheel her in a chair to hear the Word of God preached in the local school.

Over the hills at Stratherrick there lived another worthy Christian who, in some ways, resembled Hugh MacKenzie. His name was Donald MacGillivray. A few hours before Donald passed away I saw him in a hospital in Inverness. All the fears which had sometimes distressed his soul were now gone forever. His sky was like a morning without a cloud. When I asked him how he was, he went on repeating in his native Gaelic the words — "everlasting joy, everlasting joy" ("sonas siorriudh, sonas siorriudh"). On the warm lap of this great assurance and hope a smile settled on his face which even death failed to remove. The minister — the Rev. Ewan MacQueen — who prayed at Donald's funeral service used words which had their echo in some hearts present: "Lord, many of those whom we loved on earth are now with Thyself in Glory, and we long to be with them . . . "

It was in Fort Augustus that I had one of my first vivid experiences of God, by His Word, comforting me in "the night watches." The words which left their flavour in my soul ever since were:

"Thou wilt me show the path of life:
Of joys there is full store
Before Thy face; at Thy right hand
Are pleasures ever more." (Ps. 16).

I was then standing on the threshold of life as a minister of the Gospel — a life which, I soon discovered, has its own peculiar trials, anxieties and frustrations. These words came also to me wrapped in music such as I seldom heard in this world. This staff of comfort the Lord graciously placed, as it were, in my hand as I was entering upon my life's work.

About this time, also, I was sitting one day on a green slope overlooking the village of Kilmonivaig where I was conducting preparatory communion services. In the quiet calm of that summer day I heard in a voice of exquisite melody a man singing the twenty-third Psalm in the old traditional style. As the Psalm came wafting toward me from the vale below I felt the unspeakable consolation of being under the care of Him who keeps His Israel in every age.

At Glenmoriston, I sometimes looked with wonder at the famous "footprints" near Torgoyle. A hundred and seventy summers have now passed since the famous lay preacher, Finlay Munro, stood there and predicted that, as a proof that his words were from Heaven, his footprints would be seen there by successive generations. And there they are, miraculously preserved by the God whom this apostolic preacher loved so well. Finlay Munro was a man who went forth in the power of Elias calling men out of darkness into the kingdom of light. This sign in the earth is a witness against the errors of the Roman Catholic system which he so often, and on that day, exposed. It is also a sign that the Bible, which he always held in his hand, is the everlasting Word of God.

The men who ministered in other days in that beautifully situated little church at Fort Augustus, were eminent men of God. Mr Francis MacBean and Mr Alexander MacColl were men whose work the Lord had owned. For theological depth and pulpit power there were few in his generation, who could compare with Alexander MacColl. The church where he preached was to many a Bethel on Earth. And the afterglow of those days of power seemed to remain there long after the men were gone. There was, for example, an excellent woman in the district, Miss Annie Mason by name — who, like Anna of old, remained there night and day. There were seasons when, like her, I could say: "How amiable are thy tabernacles, O Lord of hosts." One of my successors there, Mr William MacLeod, was so deeply attached to that spot that, like Mr MacBean, he wished his bones to be within a few yards of its walls. Mr Macleod was a man who was "lovely" both in his life and death.

In Fort Augustus, my beloved wife and I mourned over the death of our first child. A few years after this bereavement I was at a Communion in Dores, near Inverness. One day while there, I walked up a quiet hillside road from which I thought I could see far across Loch Ness toward the place where our child's body lay. Overcome by a flood of grief all I could do was to turn my weeping eyes to God and say, "Thy Will be done." To these words I added in all sincerity, "And I bless Thy Name that Thy Will, and not our own, shall be done." No sooner did I whisper those trembling words than I became aware of another Presence. For a moment I was filled with awe, but presently this gave way to a sence of unutterable comfort. A ray of holy light fell upon my spirit. It also appeared to surround me like a luminous and warm light. It was then also that a Voice seemed to speak out of the stillness: "In my Father's House are many mansions: if it were not so I would have told you." These words I truly heard. I then knew that it was well with the child, and that by God's grace I would see him again in the Place where tears are unknown. This was indeed a happy hour, the blessedness of which remained with me for many days.

Another memory of those days was that of visiting Mr Angus A. Macdonald, minister at Strontian in Argyll. Mr Macdonald was a man of much devotional fervour, who in his experimental and warm preaching had a distinct preference for the Psalms, the Song of Solomon and the Gospel according to John. After arriving on the Saturday afternoon at the Manse to assist at his Communion, I instantly felt that "the Lord was there." The melting enjoyment of God's presence was so real that during the time we were at the Church preparing for the Lord's Table I, at least, was awed into silence through the overshadowing of the Eternal.

A similar sense of God's overpowering nearness I once felt at our Manse gate in Fort Augustus. I was at the time saying farewell to the godly Donald MacPherson, Glenurquhart, along with Mr Norman Matheson, minister at Kilmorack. My recollection is that Mr Hugh Mackenzie was there also. These brethren are long since together in their eternal Home where the enjoyment of God's face and love remain everlastingly unclouded.

Shortly before I left Glenmoriston I preached one evening in Inverness. There was a person present at the service that night who had been so deeply moved by the Word of God that outside the Church, in the hearing of many people, he proclaimed his intention to give up from that hour his sinful life and to follow the Lord. The following day this man was killed on his way home to the Western Isles. It appears that at the eleventh hour he was plucked as a brand from the burning.

Apart from the death of our child, our four years among the kind people of this lovely Highland Glen are, in retrospect, like a very pleasant dream. Many an hour since then do I go back in memory to those days, and to those choice men and women who, by a life and conversation becoming the Gospel, graced this lower vale, but most of whom now inhabit that blessed Place where death and separation are unknown.

Chapter Six

THE BELOVED VOICE

IN AUGUST 1934 we left our beloved Glenmoriston for Glasgow. I had been called to minister to the young — and at that time somewhat disturbed — congregation of Partick Highland Church.

My predecessor in Partick was the Rev. Peter M. Chisholm who afterwards became minister of Lochalsh in Ross-shire. Mr Chisholm was truly a man of God. Throughout his ministerial life his easily disturbed mind alternated between light and shade, between wind and calm. There were seasons in his life, however, when he could emerge out of his spiritual perplexities and preach the Gospel with great composure, and with much power and effect. Theologically he was exact and profound, while his own Christian experience, which had touched both the depths and the heights, enabled him to minister comfort to God's afflicted people.

The Rev. John MacLeod, who in those days ministered in Hope Street Free Church, was with me in the pulpit on my first Sabbath in Glasgow. His solemn sermon on that occasion was, if I remember rightly, based on the words of Psalm Eleven: "If the foundations be destroyed what can the righteous do." Mr MacLeod was a man of ability, of transparent character and of a kindly disposition. In my boyhood days in Lewis his name — "MacLeoid Urraidh" — was a household word throughout the island. To the end he was a man who commanded the affection and respect of the Lord's people wherever he laboured.

Life in the city has both its difficulties and compensations. The unending round of activities often fray the nerves and exhaust the body. The annual rest in the country, however, does much to restore one to a normal tone.

In the month of July, in the following year, we went for a rest to the Island of Arran. We had hardly settled down in our wayside cottage there than my wife took ill. That summer day, full of anxiety and foreboding, I entered another apartment where a Bible lay on the table. With a prayer on my lips I took it in my hand while I asked God to comfort me in my fear. In some real way I felt urged, as by another voice, to open the Book and read. The words on which my eyes rested were those of Psalm 128.

> "Blessed is every one that feareth the Lord, that walketh in His ways. For thou shalt eat the labour of thy hands: happy shalt thou be, and it shall be well with thee.
>
> Thy wife shall be a fruitful vine by the sides of thine house: thy children shall be like olive plants round about thy table. Behold, that thus shall the man be blessed that feareth the Lord. The Lord shall bless thee out of Zion, and thou shalt see the good of Jerusalem all the days of thy life. Yea, thou shalt see thy children's children, and peace upon Israel."

When I read these words I felt like one on the fringe of a world of infinite blessedness. A sense of indescribable consolation filled my heart. This, I felt certain, was the inheritance God gave me. My faith leaped for joy and grasped every precious syllable of the Psalm. I then told my wife that all would be well and that her life was to be prolonged and preserved.

That month I could not walk by shore or stream without letting my eyes feast on that Psalm. It became the subject of my song. I had a deep feeling that blessings lay hid within its several promises which had to do not only with this present life but with the life to come. The Psalm brought me to the portals of that place where peace shall forever reign through righteousness. Satan and sin have often tried to rob me of this treasure which I found that day in the field of Scripture. But God has enabled me to hold on to it in every situation and trial. I have lived to see its promises, within the sphere of Providence, fulfilled. How can I then doubt but that, when I leave this scene of time, I shall get the remainder?

Only for those secret refreshings I would have fainted in my work. When first I began my work as a young minister I had cherished the pleasant illusion that all professing Christians would surely exert themselves in God's cause. How soon did the illusion fade! I had formed this some-somewhat innocent belief by reading of the Christians of former days when the Church was awake and alive. But in an age of abounding iniquity and much spiritual decline the love of many had waxed cold. And where love to Christ is feeble, interest in His cause is bound to die.

My greatest burden, however, was myself. I felt that I lived a lean spiritual life, and that I had not weeded out of my life those things which retard one's growth in grace and impede one's usefulness in the Lord's work. In this burdened condition I went the following year to Strachur in Argyll. Ever blessed be the Lord: while quietly resting there, He favoured me with a Bethel season and a time of love.

One night, in Strachur, as a weight of sin and its sorrow sensibly pressed upon my spirit, I retired to my bedroom to pray. Immediately I closed the door I felt like a helpless captive in the grasp of an unseen foe. The inaudible cry which had gone from my soul in that hour must have been heard in Heaven. For as I stood there with my eyes lifted up to God I was given a wonderful sense of deliverance and peace.

Standing before an open window, through which streamed the warm air of the summer evening, my whole inward being came instantly under this reviving light and heavenly love. For two weeks afterwards I walked in the light of Christ's face and with my soul bathed in His love. The words of the Bride in the Song I often whispered to myself: "I charge you, oh ye daughters of Jerusalem, by the roes, and by the hinds of the field, that you stir not up, nor awake my love, till He please . . ."

I trust I had days of communion with the Lord before then, but there was a depth and a constancy in this enjoyment which surpassed anything I had hitherto experienced. This was a drink that went down sweetly, causing my lips literally to speak in sleep. It was Heaven indeed to open my eyes in the night and say, "My Beloved is mine."

During this season I wanted to be much alone. I held converse with the Lord Jesus as with a Friend. I climbed solitary hills and took quiet walks where I could escape the presence of men, especially those who were destitute of grace and spiritual sympathy.

But this good day could not endure. The sun went slowly down, but its afterglow remained with me for many days. The memory of this happy season is still both sweet and sad. In that beloved Argyllshire village I dwelt for a season in the suburbs of Heaven.

During those seasons of consolation it seemed to me that a new beauty clothed all the works of God. There are those who profess to see grandeur and beauty in nature, but whose eyes are blind to the glory of the Lord. But no one truly sees loveliness in nature but those who first see the loveliness of God Himself. The starry heavens are more friendly, and take on a new significance, when we look upon them as the work of His fingers. The sea with its roar; the silence of the everlasting hills; the placid lake with its calm reflections; the varied colourings and fragrance of flowers; the singing brooks and the song of the birds — all these are more wonderful to Christian eyes than to others. Those who are reconciled to God and in communion with Him are consciously living in a friendly universe. The pictures they see on the wall of nature are dear to them since they are the creations of Him who is altogether lovely.

But the Christian makes little of visible and created glories since they are comparatively dim "by reason of the glory that excelleth," and which is manifested in the Person and work of the Lord. It is not in the mirror of nature that we see the beauty of Christ but in the glass of his own Word. The vision of faith alone enlightens, and brings with it a joy which is unspeakable and full of glory.

The unusualness of such experiences as these, and the manner in which they almost invariably take one "by surprise," is probably the reason why they make such a deep impression on the mind and heart and stand out with such unfading clarity in one's memory. Let me here give one or two other instances of this.

Once I was asked to assist at a communion. The congregation was large, and at a time of bodily weakness, the exertion required to sustain the 'Action' service filled me with concern. But the Lord calmed my mind. Early on Sabbath morning I awoke as if someone had whispered these words in my ear: "In the midst of the Church I will sing praise unto Thee." Peace filled my heart and with Jacob I could say, "Surely the Lord is in this place."

My theme that day was the love and the sufferings of Christ. While the people were singing, and before I arose to preach, I remembered that God caused a 'deep sleep' to fall upon Adam before he took his bride and wife out of his side. When he awoke out of that peaceful and painless slumber he saw Eve, in all her loveliness, at his side. It was not so with the second man from Heaven. When God took the very life and salvation of His Bride out of His pierced side He remained fully conscious of all those agonies which rent His soul and body. Did He not say in that hour:

> "I all My bones may tell; they do
> Upon me look and stare?"

When later on I touched upon this thought the spiritual atmosphere in the church seemed to change and a hush came over the people. Many wept. The awe of the Eternal seemed to rest on all present. The awareness of God's presence was such that for a time I could not speak. That day the Lord, I hope, enabled me to show forth His praise. The morning promise He had fulfilled. From that hour I began more particularly, and with greater care, to mark God's Word when thus taking possession of my mind — whether awake or asleep. The words of Solomon — "When thou awakest it shall talk with thee," (Prov. 6), have assumed a new meaning in my life.

Another such incident I may mention. I was present at the time at another Communion. On Saturday evening my wife told me over the telephone that I was a "smallpox contact" and that the Health Authorities were anxious to trace me. Before leaving home I had visited a hospital to which this deadly infection had been traced. The thought that I had brought misery, and perhaps death, to some of the people to whom I ministered filled me with a great fear. In the Manse there was a little fair-haired girl who, now and again, invaded the minister's study. Did I become a messenger of death to this little one who had smiled at my side? As this fear was settling on my mind I heard, like the chimes of a distant bell, the words — "My foot standeth in an even place: in the congregations will I bless the Lord" (Ps. 26). The words announced that the plague had not touched me, and that the coming day would bring us a blessing.

There was another hour in my life when, beset by a sore trial, the Lord delivered me in a strange way. In a dream one night a dear minister of Christ, then at his rest in Heaven, came into a room where I was sitting alone. He had the Bible open in his hand. To my amazement he began to preach. When he had ended his heart-melting sermon I awoke, but of all that he said I could recall nothing except the verse of Scripture with which he ended: "And the God of peace shall bruise Satan under your feet shortly." When I awoke I came to realise that, whatever form they may take, our afflictions here are light and only for a moment, and that the Lord will not suffer us to be tempted beyond what we are able to endure.

During another season of bodily weakness I was greatly helped by the words — "Cast thy burden upon the Lord and He shall sustain thee." (Ps. 55). In a strange way, and in the night watches, I was reminded that the word 'burden' in the original Hebrew also meant 'a gift'. This meaning I found to be correct. As if all our heavy burdens were but the disguised blessings of the all-wise Father of our spirits! As if each dreaded cloud were big with mercies! The following Lord's Day at a Communion in Inverness-shire I felt, as I was beginning to preach, such an accession of strength passing through my frame as made me realise anew that as the vast universe around us is upheld by the Word of His power, so the trembling souls who trust in the Lord are upheld by that same Word.

In making mention of such experiences as these I know that some would object to any reliance even on Scripture as unsafe and foolish unless it is conveyed to us during our conscious hours when the mind is normal and capable of rational activity. But Scripture, as I believe, does not exclude the possibility of God communicating His mind to His people during the hours of sleep as He does during the hours of conscious existence. The Bible, in fact, affirms that He does this. Was not Jacob nearer to God in his Bethel dream than at any other time in his life? There also he listened to God's voice as He blessed him.

Such manifestations are also a characteristic of the New Testament dispensation as well as of the Old. And we live in that dispensation now.

There are others who might say that it is contrary to Scripture to believe in "mere dreams" even when they come within the context of God's holy Word. If, however, we concede, as we must, that God did in other ages use such means as one way — however subordinate and secondary — of elucidating and interpreting His Providence and of communicating His grace and presence to the soul, the question arises as to whether this door of converse or communion with the unseen world is now closed. Has He, in fact, ceased to speak to men, and especially to His own people, in this way? Has He closed this door through which He imparted His secrets to His people in other ages — both in the Old and New Testament times? No. He keeps all His doors open, this one included.

Were we to say that He has closed this door, we should not only deny that the Christian believer is spiritually in touch with the supernatural world of glory, but we should also contradict the overwhelming consensus of belief within the Christian Church, as this is reflected not only in the Gospels but also in Christian biography. Christian biography in every age gives innumerable instances of such communications. The subjects of these never questioned their significance, nor that they were vividly written on the mind and heart by the finger of God. One could speak of the "dreams" of such normal but eminently godly persons as John Newton, William Huntington, Philip Dodridge, John Howe, John Bunyan, Christmas Evans, John Kennedy, Francis MacBean, Hector MacPhail, Mrs Fletcher, the Duchess of Gordon, Madame Guyon and many others besides.

None of those whom I have mentioned would ever presume to ask God to show them His mind in this way. They were men and women who went to Heaven with the Word of God in their hand and in their heart. God's Word was the light which guided them on the way Home. When, however, in His sovereign wisdom, and in confirmation of His promise, the Lord sealed instruction on their hearts in this way they were glad of His guidance and care.

In Bunyan's "Pilgrim's Progress" we are told of Mercy's beautiful dream which made her laugh in her sleep. When she awoke, Christian reminded her that "we need not to lie awake in bed to talk with God. He can visit us while we sleep, and cause us then to hear His voice. Our heart oftentimes wakes while we sleep; and God can speak to us either by words, by signs and similitudes as well as if one is awake." Bunyan is here speaking objectively and at the bar of Scripture. He quotes the words of Job: "For God speaketh once, yea twice, yet man perceiveth it not. In a dream, in a vision of the night, when deep sleep falleth upon men . . . Then he openeth the ears and sealeth their instruction."

Speaking personally, there were times when I could not but wonder if such Scriptural impressions — such as I have mentioned — were really God speaking to my soul in answer to prayer. An unbelieving heart would sometimes insinuate that it was not wise to place any reliance on God's Word which came to me while I was still asleep. But now like many of His people I know that God has often spoken to me in this mysterious way. I have also learned that the Lord does not dispense His gold with an unjudicious hand. His answers come, not only in season, but sweetly appropriate to our state at the time. Never "in the night watches" did I find the Word of the Lord in my mouth but in answer to prayer, and as the arrow of the Lord's deliverance in some trial, or of exhortation or encouragement in some duty.

A man who greatly reassured me on this subject of spiritual converse with God was the saintly "Rabbi" Duncan, whose able and helpful analysis of the meaning of assurance is perfectly consistent with Scripture. "If there is as much reality in God speaking to man as there is in man speaking to God, then as certainly as the believer has access by the Spirit through Christ unto the Father in presenting his supplication, so certainly the Father has access through the Son by the Spirit that dwells in the new man to convey His answer. Given a spiritual world, a living God and a living soul, is it incredible that there should be such intercourse between them; that the soul should speak to a hearing God and hear a speaking God? This, indeed, is the very kernel of experimental religion. Now, to enjoy full assurance we need a particular saying of God to our souls — 'Say unto my soul, I am thy salvation.'"

Dr John Kennedy of Dingwall in his great sermon on "The secret of the Lord," shows that this "prophetic" element which enriches the Christian experience of many believers has been continuous within the true Church of God from the beginning. "A mere nominal Christian," he says, "is a stranger to such intimations of the Lord's will by the special application of God's Word. He thinks that in his approach to the Hearer of prayer the speaking is all on his own side. But it is otherwise with those who truly fear the Lord. It is when they hear the Lord's voice speaking to themselves that they can venture to utter words of faith and hope. Their prayer is, 'Cause me to hear thy loving kindness in the morning, for in Thee do I trust.' 'Be not silent unto me.' His own people speak to Him about His doings and He speaks to them. Shall they not, therefore, know the bearing of His providence as others cannot? Shall not such, by His Word thus given, penetrate, as with a seer's eye, a future which is all dark to others, while in all truth and honesty they may claim to be "neither a prophet nor the son of a prophet." They are little acquainted with God, as the godly Dr Love remarked, who think that He has ceased to give His people assurance as to future events. God has not bound Himself in this manner; and there have been many things intimated and made known to some of His people before such things came to pass.

"Those who dismiss all kinds of intercourse with the Invisible God as a claim to the gift of prophecy or as faith in dreams and visions, and who speak of those who claim the privilege of communion with God as deluded fanatics, should remember that the standing ground of their hope ever is — 'Thus saith the Lord'."

I spoke earlier of the days of my youth when in our home in the Island of Lewis I used to listen to the chaste conversation of godly men and women. The oft recurring phrase — "God in His Word recently awoke me out of sleep" was to me in those days both strange and mysterious. To them it expressed a well-known spiritual enjoyment, the reality of which not one of them doubted. They were a people who knew the way to the Throne of grace, and who cast all their cares upon the God in whom they trusted. When in His court they presented their plea they knew that He would answer in His own time and way. If, as He sometimes did, He remained silent they knew that it was His glory "to conceal a thing." His "No" was an answer as well as His "Yes."

Often, indeed, have I wondered at the nearness which those simple believers in the Lord enjoyed. What did it mean? Some in this age would try to explain such experiences, in terms of association, extra-sensory perception, suggestibility, the momentary removal of the "Time Barrier," or the emergence into the conscious mind of those repressed fears and desires which lie in the deeper subconscious self. But true Christian experience shall always remain outwith the reach of mere human penetration. This is what God insists on in His word. "Eye hath not seen, ear hath not heard, neither hath it entered into the heart of man what God hath prepared for them who love Him, and which are now revealed to us by the Holy Spirit." In this matter God's rejection of the wisdom of this world, however learned and advanced in its own eyes, is utterly final, if not contemptuous. "But the natural man receiveth not the things of the Spirit of God, for they are foolishness unto him, neither can he know them, for they are spiritually discerned."

This "encounter" with God through His Word and in answer to prayer has often brought me to a standstill at the thought of His sovereign condescension in conversing with men whose feet are in the dust. The implication of this experience is far reaching in its wonder. It means that God is ever present with His people. He truly dwells in their hearts by faith, and by whispering His secrets into their hearts, He fills their sky with stars which anticipate the coming day. His unchangeableness in His love and in His promise is what gives consistency to all true Christian experience. The spiritually quickened live in "the heavenlies," or in a dimension of existence beyond space and time. And this converse with God in Christ is an invaluable Christian apologetic which doubt and atheism can never gainsay. It is also something which they can never understand nor believe.

But this is a subject on which we need not dwell, for I suppose that many of the Lord's people could tell of unusual happenings of this nature over which, like another, they ponder in their hearts. And if many of them do not have such experiences as these, their daily coming to God in prayer, for the bread of life and the needed grace, are as great an evidence of being the Lord's as any other.

But this is a subject on which we need not dwell. To suppose that many of the [illegible] people [illegible] [illegible] [illegible] [illegible] an evidence of being the Lord's as any other.

Chapter Seven

THE GATHERING STORM

DURING those years the German military power was on the ascendant in Europe. A whole continent trembled before the harsh threatening voice of Adolf Hitler. It looked as if nothing could save Europe from the ever-lengthening shadow of this Teutonic menace with its cruel emphasis on a policy of the destruction of the Jews, and, indeed, of all "inferior" races.

Like others I was concerned about the survival of our nation. The day France fell I could, humanly speaking, see no protection for our own country except in the blue band of sea which surrounded our island nation. When, however, I knelt in prayer and sought God's intervention in the matter, I was directed to that passage in the Book of Psalms: "And Who hath redeemed us from our enemies, for His mercy endureth forever." (Ps. 136, 24).

The following Lord's Day I felt encouraged to ask the people to look to God Who had thus promised deliverance and victory to our nation. Some who 'walked by sight' thought I had spoken unadvisedly, as to all appearances we had already lost the war. But the Lord had spoken, and in His Word I rested.

On that memorable Sabbath morning in 1939 when Britain had declared war on Germany I was in the Island of Coll conducting Communion services where my friend, the Rev. John Newall, was minister. Nearly all present at the service were aware of what had taken place, except myself. The minister wisely kept the news from me till after the holy ordinance had been observed. After the service we sat in the manse. On the distant horizon one could see a darkness gathering, laden with the portents of a great storm. The wind began to rise, and the lightning, followed by reverberating thunder, rent the dark cloud. It looked like a symbol of the death dealing storm which was shortly to affect the lives of millions of helpless human beings on this planet. Only this was the kinder voice of nature, and not the terrifying tempest of destruction unleashed on the world by sinful men.

As the storm died away on the distant deep, one remembered the words:

> "The voice of the Lord is upon the waters; the God of glory thundereth: the Lord is upon many waters...
> The Lord sitteth upon the flood; yea, the Lord sitteth King for ever.
> The Lord will give strength unto His people; the Lord will bless His people with peace." (Psalm 29).

In the summer of 1941 when Germany was flushed with the prospect of an early victory, General Franco of Spain made a speech in which he said that it was "a mathematical certainty" that Germany would win the war. He therefore advised the Allies to give up the struggle. It was not difficult to discern that behind his words loomed the shadow of the Vatican which had pronounced its sordid benedictions over the Fascist swords.

The morning I read those words of Franco, I wrote a hurried letter to the Press which contained the following words:

> "General Franco's assertion to the effect that the Allies are losing the war makes interesting reading....
>
> The British Empire is not going to lose the war.... The time of our deliverance I cannot tell, but that Hitler will never succeed in imposing his Satanic 'new order' on the world, or even on Europe, is a thing which Eternal Providence has decreed... Britain shall survive. For this let God be praised in the certain anticipation of it."

This letter appeared the following day — July 21st, 1941 — in "The Glasgow Herald." One man denounced me severely in cold print, since according to him it was obvious that Germany was already victorious.

About the same time I ventured to write Mr Winston Churchill a more studied letter in which I repeated my strong conviction that, under his hand, God would bring the nation out of its great peril. Mr Churchill, through his private secretary, warmly thanked me for my encouraging word.

In the summer of 1940 I went to England to preach to Highland sailors at Plymouth and Portsmouth. Germany had not, as yet, launched its attacks on the cities of our country. In the south of England, however, the weird sounds of the sirens would, night after night, break the stillness of a summer night or early morning.

In Portsmouth I had my first experience of a severe air-raid on the Naval barracks there. On a cloudless day, as I was walking into the naval quarters, a warning was sounded. We had hardly entered the subterranean tunnel beneath the Square than huge quantities of mud and debris poured over us. Wandering about in the intricate network of trenches I came across two young men from my native Island. They were alone. There I lifted up my thoughts in silent prayer to God. When at last we emerged into the light of day the place had been churned up almost beyond recognition, all of which happened within a short time.

Before this ordeal these words powerfully impressed themselves on my mind. "Ascribe ye strength unto God. His excellency is over Israel, and His strength is in the clouds." (Ps. 68.34). The words, I knew, contained an assurance of safety under the wings of the Eternal.

During my stay at Plymouth I was privileged to see one of the happiest death-beds I had ever attended. It was that of a young Highland sailor. Besides the joy which radiated from this lad's face one could see that his lines had fallen in a pleasant place, and that he was already on the fringe of the world of glory. In this wonderful frame he passed out of time.

It was on a clear and lovely night in 1941 that the German bombers made a devastating attack on Clydeside. I was in the act of pronouncing the blessing in our Church Hall in Glasgow after a service when the warning came. That night the moon was full, the weather mild, and the stars, so bright and peaceful, seemed unusually near and kindly.

Perhaps that was because the silent universe, though wrapped in mystery, appeared friendly in contrast to what at that hour was happening in our sin-sick world.

When I arrived home my wife was preparing to move the children to a corner of one of our cellar rooms. Our boy, then a mere child, had an idea that all the noise outside was created for his own special entertainment! With the crash of each distant bomb he would look up and smile. This infant and innocent illusion wrung my heart. He had entered a cruel and fallen world but as yet he knew it not.

The following week I moved the family to our beloved Glenmoriston while I remained with my flock in Glasgow. During those sad days, when Death on dark wings moved over our heads, the Lord kept reassuring me of His protection in these words: "There shall no evil befall thee, neither shall any plague come nigh thy dwelling; for He shall give His angels charge concerning thee, to keep thee in all thy ways." (Ps. 91).

On a subsequent occasion, awakened out of sleep by a raid warning, He reassured me in these words — "Wait on the Lord and keep His way, and He shall exalt thee to inherit the land; when the wicked are cut off, thou shalt see it." (Ps. 37). These precious truths were sent to remind us of the unfailing care of the Redeemer whether we tarried in the city or lodged in a quiet Highland Glen.

When in 1945 news came of Japan's defeat and the final end of the Second World War, I was in Strathpeffer. That night as I listened to a man address a crowd in the village Square, a painful apprehension settled on my mind that the storm of war had only abated for a time.

A few days afterwards, at a service of thanksgiving in my congregation in Glasgow, I was compelled to dwell on the words: "The second woe is past, and behold the third woe cometh quickly."

Not long after this I passed through a very solemn experience in my sleep. Out of that troubled sleep I awoke quoting the words of a Psalm.

"And then the heavens shall declare
His righteousness abroad;
Because the Lord Himself doth come,
None else is judge but God." (Ps. 50).

Those words were in my mouth, but it seemed to me also as if their thunder was reverberating through the whole world. With this voice went a very vivid dream. Before I awoke I dreamt I was in one of our Scottish cities. The evening was calm and bright, and thousands moved unconcernedly on its streets. In a moment the skies darkened as if the shadow of something unutterably dreadful had fallen on the land. It came bearing upon the city — an avalanche of destruction from which there was no escape. I saw the city being swept away by an inconceivable horror of fire and storm. The utter helplessness of man in such a cataclysm of destruction made me tremble. Ever since that night I have never stood on the streets of that famous and historic city — which is also a city of "festivals" and entertainments — without being deeply awed by those dread events which lie hidden in the womb of Providence, but which, in the appointed time, must surely come to pass. A few years afterwards, and during one of my ecclesiastical visits to this city, I retired one night to rest. In the early morning I awoke deeply awed by words from the same Psalm:

"Before Him fire shall waste, great storms
Shall compass Him about."

This confirmation of God's Word made me tremble. I also felt that these dread prophetic words of Holy Scripture had reference to more than one of the cities of this fallen world.

Because I believe that God shall fulfil His Word, I also believe that "His strange work" is not yet over. We live, in fact, in a deeply imperilled world.

On the 6th of August, 1945, I was sitting in the Cockburn Hotel in Edinburgh, when a voice came over the air. "The revelation of the secrets of nature, long mercifully withheld from men, should arouse the most solemn reflections in the mind and conscience of every human being capable of comprehension." It was exactly 9 o'clock in the evening when these words of Mr Winston Churchill fell on the ears of the nation.

The words were related to the destruction of two Japanese cities that morning by two atomic bombs. From the United States we were at the same moment reminded that "man has succeeded in harnessing the basic power of the universe . . . ."

On that very morning, in the ruins of Hiroshima, a young Christian minister read the following words from the Bible to a dying Japanese:

"Thou turnest man to destruction; and sayest, Return, ye children of men. For a thousand years in Thy sight are but as yesterday when it is past, and as a watch in the night. Thou carriest them away as with a flood: they are as a sleep: in the morning they are like grass which groweth up. In the morning it flourisheth, and groweth up: in the evening it is cut down, and withereth.

For we are consumed in Thine anger, and by Thy wrath are we troubled. Thou has set our iniquities before Thee, our secret sins in the light of Thy countenance. For all our days are passed away in Thy wrath: we spend our years as a tale that is told." (Ps. 90).

These words pointed to God's red light of future danger, but, as subsequent events proved, man deliberately shut his eyes to God's warning and turned his ears from God's plea to return to righteousness and to obey His Will as it is revealed in the Holy Scriptures.

One could not therefore fail to see that another and a greater storm was gathering on the world horizon. With the passing of the years it became more and more evident that escape was impossible, and that mankind was entangled in the deep snare of their own sin. The growing and universal apprehension of danger brought many significant reactions. A Godless generation began to clamour for the banning of all nuclear weapons of war, while "the cry" of their sin, like that of Sodom, had reached the ear of God.

The great tragedy of all, and the most ominous sign of our rapid and terrifying moral and spiritual deterioration, is seen in the way in which many of our leaders, in different spheres, condone, and approve of, the sins which bring upon men God's righteous indignation. Sodomy, gambling, abortion, the destruction of the Lord's Day, immorality, the removal of the death penalty, with masses of filfth pouring out from our cinemas, theatres, on television, radio and literary media as "the done thing" in a censorless, permissive society have brought us, as a nation, to the point of no return. Soon God's Word shall be fulfilled:—

"How in a moment suddenly
  to ruin brought are they!
With fearful terrors utterly
  they are consumed away." (Ps. 73).

"Snares, fire and brimstone, furious storms,
  on sinners He shall rain:
This, as the portion of their cup,
  doth unto them pertain." (Ps. 11).

These are not the predictive words of mere man, but the words of the God who cannot lie. And these fears are not that of a morbid pessimist, but of many others of God's people today, who have the same "inside information" with regard to the dread processes of God's holy providence in the not-far-away future.

To the dear people of God, living, as they do, in such an age, the sweetest word of all is: "The Lord doth reign." He Who makes "all things work together for their good" is "God over all and blessed forever." All the saints are in His hand, and "as the mountains are about Jerusalem so is the Lord round about His people." God protected His people in other ages from the perils to which they were exposed. "He suffered no man to do them wrong: yea, He reproved kings for their sakes, saying, Touch not mine anointed, and do my prophets no harm." If for an ungodly world there is, as in the days of Noah, no place to hide, God, in His own way, will keep His own people in every trial, and from His love neither life nor death can separate them. "For your life is hid with Christ in God."

Chapter Eight

THE ANOINTED PILLAR

ONE EARLY morning in Glasgow I suddenly collapsed through overwork. Lying low in the utter weakness of physical exhaustion a cloud overshadowed my spirit. The Enemy, taking advantage of my condition, began again to rejoice over me and to suggest to my mind that my days on earth were over and that my purposes were broken off.

At family worship one night, I asked my wife to "read anywhere." The Bible opened at the seventy-first Psalm. When she read the words, "Oh God, forsake me not, until I have showed Thy strength to this generation, and Thy power to everyone that is to come," I was much troubled. Hitherto, I felt, I had done nothing for the One Who had done so much for me. Behind me lay a lean life of poor unprofitable service. Would He in mercy spare me, that, by His good hand upon me, I might still serve Him before I left the world? That night I nearly wept my remaining strength away.

After some time the doctor deemed me fit to travel to Glenmoriston. There the wholesome heather-scented air from the hills acted like a balm on my enfeebled frame. But for many days my soul pined in the absence of a fresh blessing and in longing for the conscious enjoyment of the Lord's face. My prayers seemed to freeze on my lips, and spiritually speaking I was like one who had long been dead.

One calm night I stood at the door of our cottage looking at the lovely moonlit sky. Across the Moriston river a wreath of white mist encircled, like a halo, one of the nearer hills. The river flowed gently between two meadows. A mantle of peace appeared to have fallen on the world. Only "the God of peace," I mused, could form such a scene.

For a few moments I tried to envisage a world without its present terrifying conflicts, wars and sorrows. I began to picture in my own mind what our sin-stricken and war-torn world would be like during the glory of the latter days.

It was then that something inconceivably blissful and overpowering dropped into my soul. Like a leaf from the Tree of Life it brought instant healing and reviving to my spirit. Looking up, and with the inner eye, I saw 'Him that sitteth upon the Throne.' The love of Christ I felt flooding my heart, and I enjoyed a fresh view of His glory as the First and the Last. In a moment my cup was full and running over. My soul was drawn up to God and by means of an awakened love for Him, and the exercise of a quickened faith, I felt I had the power, as I had the desire, to draw Him through the very clouds into my heart. "My Lord and my God" was all that my soul could utter. As there was something "unspeakable" in this enjoyment I can only describe its more immediate effects on my spirit.

My first urge was to praise God and to admire Him in all His works. Whether I thought of His creation, providence, or redemptive work, I could see nothing but perfection stamped on the whole. I admired Him especially as the God of Holiness Who had come out of His place to punish the heathen who had not known Him, and the nations which had not called on His name (Psalm 79). The God whose strong hand was stretched out in indignation over this world I could justify and praise. My soul danced before the view I enjoyed of Him who went forth "conquering and to conquer." "The Lord at thy right hand shall strike through Kings in the day of His wrath . . . He shall drink of the brook in the way, therefore shall He lift up the head." (Psalm 110). "Great and marvellous are thy works, Lord God Almighty; just and true are Thy ways, Thou King of saints. Who shall not fear Thee, O Lord, and glorify Thy Name?" My happy spirit came under the power of many such words as these.

I had also a strong urge to wrestle with the Angel of the Covenant, who thus, I believed, honoured me with His presence. The burden of my prayer was the revival of His Zion, and the exertion of "the exceeding greatness of His power" to raise her again from the dust, and to clothe her in fresh power and beauty. I also found it easy to pray for the destruction of the kingdom of darkness and for the removal of the deep idolatries which defile the world and which bring countless souls down to perdition.

There was a quiet and secret spot not far from our cottage where sheep had made a track through the bell heather. By this green path there was a small rock which jutted out of the ground. Night after night I paced this path. Sometimes I would kneel by the stone as if anointing the pillar with my tears. I was shut up to the one plea — "For Zion's sake I will not hold my peace . . . . " Rays from the Sun of Righteousness also gladdened my soul for many days. Christ and He alone filled the universe for me then. "Whom have I in heaven but Thee, and there is none upon earth that I desire beside Thee." (Psalm 73).

When at last the consolation sensibly diminished, the Tempter came to trouble me. There is a snare laid for the feet of a Christian not only in the valley of common experience but, as in the case of Paul, on the highest pinnacle of Christian enjoyment. And the snare which is set where we imagine Satan cannot follow us often proves the more dangerous. It is on the mountain top that we need to watch out footsteps. When we feel secure we become less watchful and thereby expose ourselves to the 'fiery darts' which can set the soul aflame.

The temptation took this form. Satan whispered to my soul that to praise God for permitting those awesome outbreaks of His judgements on the earth was not a Christian spirit. The true Christian ought to deplore these calamities and ask God to bring them to an end. But I knew that many who deplore the effects of sin as seen in death, sorrow and fear, never deplored or repented of the sin whch was their cause. But as God's judgement upon our personal and national sins was a reflection of His holy, just and unchangeable nature, I could not but rejoice. The fire which God rained on the cities of the plain was not the evil, but the sins of the people. His judgements are holy.

When I consulted the Bible I was very happy to see my own state of mind exactly portrayed in Isaiah, chapter 24. There I saw the contrast between a Godless world and the true Church of Christ. The former, amid natural desolation, murmured over the loss of their temporal enjoyments and security. The remnant of God's people left were of a very different spirit and conversation. "When thus it shall be in the midst of the land, among the people, there shall be as the shaking of an olive tree and as the gleaning of grapes when the vintage is done. They shall lift up their voice, they shall sing for the majesty of the Lord, they shall cry aloud from the sea." In this passage I found a sword with which I could vanquish the enemy.

When on a later occasion I revisited Glenmoriston and came within sight of what I hope was my "Peniel" I was overcome with tears by memories which, I hope, will abide with me forever.

Before I left Glenmoriston a heavy burden was placed on my conscience to write something about what I considered to be, in the light of God's Word, the more aggravating evils which had paved a way for God's indignation. This poor man's offering God, I hope, richly blessed, for, through successive editions, it was warmly received by many thousands of God's people in different parts of the world.

Ever since I began my ministry I was led to read several 'Lives' of C. H. Spurgeon. In Glenmoriston I had opportunity to read more of his excellent sermons. Like many others before me the more I read of this man and his work the more I wondered at his great powers and immense labours. The cluster of rare gifts and graces which grew on Spurgeon's branch was without compare. When, by the grace of God, Spurgeon yielded his life to Christ, the Church of God on earth could rejoice in one of the greatest gifts possibly bestowed upon her in his age. Where he excelled was in his holy love and devotion to his Lord, and in his yearning for the salvation of souls. Spurgeon is immortal, and though his star may fade somewhat in evil times he is destined to reappear throughout the coming ages in the full splendour of the glorious Gospel which he so faithfully proclaimed. And his voice was such that the like of it was seldom heard on this earth. Sometimes I used to think of those vanished multitudes who were privileged to hear the cadences of that far-reaching and heart-stirring voice. It was a great privilege to have listened to that messenger of God whose feet were so beautiful on the Gospel mountain. And here I hope I may be forgiven if I relate another of my strange dreams related to this great and much loved man.

In this dream, I recall, I found myself worshipping in a certain church in Glasgow. The service was a formal and meaningless ritual. The well-robed minister who mumbled his words out of a book wearied me so much that I turned my back on the pulpit and congregation. Thus, in the back pew, I sat facing the entrance door which was made of clear glass. In this contrary and unhappy situation the door suddenly brightened with a light which shone upon it from without. Then a plain pulpit appeared, and in it a plain-looking man whom I recognised as C. H. Spurgeon. With his hand upraised he cried in a marvellous bell-like voice, "Behold, behold, the everlasting love which God in Christ had for His Own people." It was as if the preacher desired me to enjoy a taste of this love in my own soul. Slowly the voice and vision faded, and I awoke. When I came to full consciousness I was quite melted and overcome by a sense of that sweet and unutterable love which Spurgeon proclaimed. It was pre-eminently the unspeakable enjoyment of God Himself. I remember standing on my bedroom floor and pleading with God to leave me in that state of joy and rapture for ever and ever. But alas, it was not to be — as yet. I felt like a man being let down gently from a world of infinite happiness till at last I found myself standing again in this cold world with my heart full of sin and my mind full of sorrow. Oh! how I grieved at having lost so soon what I would fain have kept within my being for ever and ever.

Looking back on that night when I was surprised by this unspeakable love and joy, I knew, in the light of God's Word, that as a human being is capable of abysmal sorrow and despair, he is also capable of a deep joy besides which the so-called pleasures and happiness of this world are both vain and empty. To possess this joy in its solidity, depth and permanence we must leave this fallen world and put off our body of death and humiliation. No man can see God's face and live. Death is the last stepping stone to this enjoyment. How wonderful is the promise that we are to enjoy Him for ever and ever.

The recollection of that night sometimes left me sad lest through my sin I should never again get this wonderful thing permanently into my heart. It will be heaven to possess it. To miss it would be to live in the deepest impoverishment and deprivation for ever. Oh! but I know that a good and just God would not tantalise us with such sweet drops from His river unless He meant us to drink out of it in a fuller measure by and by.

There were few who enjoyed more "earnests" of future happiness than Spurgeon himself. In a sermon of great tenderness and beauty he dwells on Christ manifesting Himself to His people in a way unknown to the world, and indeed, to many who think they do know Him. To those who cry out "nonsense" at the very mention of ecstasies, or the spiritual dance of the soul in communion with God, he says, "very well, you have proved yourselves to be of the world when you enjoy no such manifestations." And then, like Paul, he lifts the curtain for a moment to let us see that his own communion with the world of glory was to him a living reality. "If I," he once told his great congregation, "have not gone within an inch of the pearly gates I am not here; if I have not sometimes sniffed the incense from the censers of the glorified and heard the music of their harps I think I am not a living man. There have been seasons of ecstatic joy when I have climbed the highest mountains, and I have caught some sweet whisper from the Throne. I believe most Christians have such manifestations, and if they are much in duty and much in suffering they will have them. It is not given to all to have that portion, but to some it is, and such men know what religion means. May God teach you more of this and lead you deeper."

In our little cottage in Glenmoriston, enframed in one of our bedrooms, there was a verse of Scripture. "Draw nigh unto God, and He will draw nigh unto you." One evening on entering this room I was deeply moved by these words. They seemed to challenge my faith and to reprove my spiritual lethargy. The words embodied a great promise, the truth of which I knew had been verified in the experience of God's people in every age. At that moment the Lord, I felt, was asking me to prove Him in one of His promises. Every valid excuse was taken away. I could there and then close the door and kneel in His presence in secret. The memory of that evening shall, I hope, remain with me for ever. God touched my heart and made His face shine upon me. He whispered a word of consolation in my heart. The golden sceptre of His grace He extended to me saying — "What is thy request and what is thy desire?" He had honoured His word, for in "drawing nigh" He gave me a blessing.

In these days many books have been written on the subject of prayer. But some of these have little or nothing to say about the most important aspect of the whole subject — the way God answers our prayers. The most wonderful thing, however, about prayer is not our coming to God, but His coming to us. Prayer is great only in its answer. We may clothe our prayers in Scriptural language and follow an orthodox devotional pattern, while at the same time our prayers may be still-born, with God remaining silent and standing "afar off". There are, of course, seasons in the life of every believer when God is silent. The shadow of some unconfessed and unforsaken sin may come between us and Christ. Besides, a sovereign God has His own undisclosed reasons for not always answering our prayers. But God does answer. He is not always far away and without voice. "The God who answers . . . . let Him be God." Are there not two kinds of prayers which move the heart of God toward His own people; the prayer that is born of anguish and the prayer that is born of love and desire? The prayer of Jacob at Peniel was born of fear and sorrow of heart. The prayer of Moses for a clearer view of God's glory was born of a holy desire and an ever-deepening love to Him. God heard both. He wrestled with Jacob "and blessed him there." From the cleft of the rock Moses had a wonderful and enrapturing glimpse of the glory of Christ, the Angel of the covenant.

Thomas Goodwin uses an illustration to describe how, like lovers, Christ and His people have their trysting places where they meet together in secret and where He is to each one of His own "a little sanctuary." Abraham had his oak tree underneath whose shade he retired each day to commune with God. Is there not in the life of every true Christian some place of endearing memories "where prayer is wont to be made?"

God sometimes answers our prayers by bringing that wistful "something" into our consciousness which some have spoken of as His "smile." A ray of His love touches our heart. We enjoy His presence. We get a glimpse of His face throught the lattice of some promise. This is the moment when the grace that is in our heart opens like a flower to embrace the warmth of His love, or the refreshing dew of His grace. It is an hour of mutual enjoyment when we say — "My Beloved is mine and I am His." Sometimes in our prayers we labour to break through the cold barrier of sin which so often comes between us and God or rather do we plead that He might come over "the mountains" which separates us from the enjoyment of His presence. Then it happens. We know not how. We suddenly find ourselves within His courts, "where a day is better than a thousand." The conviction is then begotten in our soul that all our desire is before Him and that our plea will truly have its answer in His own time and way.

Many of the Lord's people have discovered that God, in the words of the Psalmist, can also answer prayer "by terrible things in righteousness."

In the book of Job, Elihu deals with this very problem of Christian suffering. He envisages a man who is determined to take a certain course along some path of concealed danger. But God arrests his footsteps, and by a severe process of affliction, He withdraws him from his purpose. With the process of pain begins the process of grace. Out of the furnace a new man emerges — a man who has learned that God's love often reaches us under the harrow of trial and grief.

In answer to prayer He can work in the reverse order. He can still the storm and send a great calm. Once I found myself in the grip of a great fear. I was not afraid of anything in the external world. I was afraid of myself and of the sinful thoughts which passed through my mind. Early one morning as I was still in much distress, I was awakened by that much loved touch and voice which had so often relieved me before. "Hitherto hath the Lord helped us." These were the words which fell like a balm on my grieved heart. My adversary had to retire before his Conqueror. Christ is not only the Beloved but also the Friend. When trouble is near He is nearer still. He is the sleepless Guardian of His own Israel, and the Brother born of adversity.

The prayers of God's people are not always answered at once. Like ships which do business in foreign climes, they may take long before they return to port but return they will, even though we may not be there to see it. Let me give one or two examples of this.

Many years ago I sat beside an elderly Christian woman who, with tears in her eyes, spoke to me about her family. From the day they were born they had been the subjects of her earnest prayers. But meantime they grew up unmindful of their Christian upbringing and following the fashion of this world. The years passed and she herself passed on to her reward in Heaven, but the seed which she had sown in tears did prosper. Her works followed her, for after her departure several members of her family became sincere followers of the Lord. Their mother's prayers had prevailed with God.

There was another day when I sat in a hospital ward holding the hand of a friend. He was dying. He was a man who had served the Lord faithfully and whose work He owned. His own family, however, were still enstranged from the things which he prized. "If," he said to a friend, "I saw but one of them in a state of grace, I should die happy." But he died with his prayers still unanswered. Several years after his death I took services in a Church in one of our cities. One of his sons led me to the pulpit; another led the praise, while yet another present — an excellent young man — was preparing for the ministry of the Gospel. The bread which he had so often cast upon the waters did return after many days.

The prayers of God's people move in wider circles than that which concerns themselves. They stretch far into future ages and embrace the whole earth. David's prayer that the glory of Christ might one day fill the whole earth and that His knowledge and praise might extend from sea to sea is still to have its glorious answer.

The power of prayer is incalculable. The prayer of Joshua arrested the normal rhythm of the solar system. "The stars in their courses fought against Sisera." His reign extends to the utmost confines of the Universe and to the tiniest grain of sand. All things are ordered for the good of His people — even things which, to our limited apprehension, appear to be against us.

Let all who pray then take heart; "for the vision is yet for an appointed time, but in the end it shall speak, and not lie: though it tarry, wait for it: because it will surely come, it will not tarry." Heaven is a place of joy where those who sow in tears shall reap in joy. And how great that joy shall be when even the small tokens of that harvest which we enjoy here make us so happy! But all the glory shall be to the One of whom it is written that He "shall see of the travail of His soul and shall be satisfied."

CHAPTER NINE

TWO SEASIDE GRAVES

IN 1947 WE VISITED my father in Skye. For fourteen years he had laboured in Waternish, where he enjoyed the love and respect of a kindly and peace-loving people. But now he was stricken in years, and I could see that his mind had lost its former alertness, and that his excellent memory was becoming a little clouded. He was entering upon the last mile of life's road. The minister whom he assisted in Skye was the excellent and well-beloved Mr Duncan Morrison, who died in Gairloch in 1966. Mr Morrison was truly "a prince and a great man in Israel." My father's affection for him never abated to the end.

One day as we sat with my father in our lodgings, one of our children came in. I quietly reminded him of the way his own mother had left her blessing to me and suggested that he, if the Lord so moved him, should bless our child also. Without another word they walked into another room where he prayed earnestly beside the child. And, I hope, it was a prayer that reached the ear of God.

A few nights after arriving in Skye we felt greatly awed and comforted by God coming wonderfully near to us in the ninety-first Psalm. The great promises, and the assurance of protection and salvation given in that Psalm, were indeed a good pillow to rest on. Not only then, but always.

When the day came that we had to take leave of my father, we all accompanied him along the hillside path leading to his place of abode. It was a calm, warm evening in July. After leaving him I sat down by the wayside at Knockbreck and watched him as he slowly went out of sight. A multitude of memories surged through my mind, knowing in my heart that we should never again walk together in this world.

In this deeply affected state the following Scripture powerfully impressed itself upon my mind: "With gladness and rejoicing shall they be brought; they shall enter into the King's palace. Instead of thy fathers shall be thy children." (Psalm 45). With these precious words the Lord comforted my spirit.

When afterwards we visited him in his own home in Lewis, we found him dying. Apart from dubious flashes of recognition he knew us not. But although very weak, he was constantly occupied in worshipping God. This he did even in his sleep. While his mind and memory had now no grasp whatever of anything related to this life, he could still sing his favourite psalms, and pray without misquoting a word of Scripture. Only God, His Word, and the love of Christ, were now real to him. All else had for ever receded.

About the time of his departure another man in the community was also dying. Lying on his death-bed this respectable and naturally kindly man went on dividing his earthly substance with much care and interest, while the things of eternity and God seemed to have no place in his thoughts. The difference between these two men, both passing into the Great Unknown, seemed to me an impressive commentary on the words, "Then shall ye return, and discern between the righteous and the wicked, between him that serveth God and him that serveth Him not." (Ma. 1.3).

My father passed out of time quoting the words, "Joy in the Holy Ghost," and repeating with great solemnity the words of David — "I will make Thy Name to be remembered in all generations." (Ps. 45).

The brief December day on which his remains were carried to the grave was bathed in summer-like weather. But my greatest comfort at that hour was that during a mile's walk to the graveyard these words were present with me: "Yea, he had power over the Angel, and prevailed." (Hosea 12). On that kindly day the tiny waves which played on the sands of his native shore seemed to welcome him to his long — but not his last — home. There, beside his beloved wife, he sleeps till the dawn of another and a better day.

When my father passed away, his old minister, the Rev. Duncan MacDougall, wrote me a letter of sympathy which contained the following words, "The February Church Record has just reached us here, and I was very sorry to read in it a notice of the death of your dear father. What fragrant memories have been revived in my breast by the thought of him, and all that he was to me during my ministry in Ness. Although we had a godly Kirk Session, every man of them outstanding, yet I might truly say that your father was a man by himself. He was well fitted for the wider sphere of labour which he was called to occupy. He came to a good old age, as a shock of corn fully ripe. He rests from his labours and his works will follow him. We have always the memory of his life and conversation to spur us on to be "followers of them who through faith and patience inherit the promises."

Some time before this bereavement the Lord appeared to me in great kindness. I was assisting at the time at a Communion in Inverness. On that solemn evening America was making a new and major experiment with the dread atomic bomb at Bikini. Only a blurred, incoherent version of what was happening reached this country. That night was truly heavy with destiny for this world. As the moments passed one felt instinctively that our world had reached one of its greatest crises.

After family worship I retired to my bedroom. No sooner had I closed the door than a soft warm, mantle of love and peace was let fall on my soul. Surprised by this sweet and sudden spiritual enjoyment I stood still. "It is the Lord," was all I could say in my inward heart. In holy awe, and with my head bowed, the Lord's presence was not only unspeakably solemn, but overpowering in its blissful effects. I went down on my knees, and remained in that posture for a while. The happy moments passed, and I was still in the embrace of God's loving arms. At last the thought occurred to me that I should retire to rest, and let my wakeful heart still retain this great blessing.

In this I might have done wrongly. I recalled the Strachur days when in the night seasons I would awake out of sleep with the Lord still consciously with me. Hoping that this might be the beginning of another such time, I retired at last to bed. But it was not to be. When at dawn I awoke the sensible Presence was gone. If such Bethel seasons are brief they are memorable and refreshing, and how wonderfully do they confirm the great affirmation: "Eye hath not seen, nor ear heard, neither have entered into the heart of man the things which God hath prepared for them who love Him. But God hath revealed them to us by His Spirit."

Another treasured memory of those days was that of entering a Church in Skye on a lovely summer evening. When the sermon was over the minister gave out the last psalm. It was then that I heard a voice which seemed to me to come from the very vestibule of Heaven. The bright vistas through which I was privileged to look that evening, as the large congregation sang, filled me with deep consolation for several days. The words sung were a call to the whole of creation to rejoice in the prospect of the coming of the Lord to judge the world and to gather His people Home.

"Let heav'ns be glad before the Lord,
and let the earth rejoice;
Let seas, and all that is therein,
cry out, and make a noise.

Let fields rejoice, and ev'rything
that springeth of the earth;
Then woods and ev'ry tree shall sing
with gladness and with mirth
Before the Lord; because He comes,
to judge the earth comes He:
He'll judge the world with righteousness,
the people faithfully." (Psalm 96).

During one of my Communion journeys I again visited the Island of Lewis. There I lodged with my younger brother, Angus. On a Sabbath evening as we were walking from the Church towards the village of South Dell where he lived, I spoke to him seriously and affectionately about the eternity which we must soon enter. Inclined at that time to agnosticism, and looking upon Scriptural Calvinism as a theology of fatalism and fixed determinism, he had, in his theological attitude, abandoned his Christian upbringing almost entirely. That evening I quietly drew his attention to the heavens above us, replete with silent witnesses to the power and glory of the Lord. "And the One," I said, "Who made all these you must one day stand before, as a responsible creature.

The reason why the Lord shall banish the wicked from His presence on the Great Day is that when He was a stranger, they took Him not in. Just what He shall do to you if you refuse Him in the overtures of His grace."

Later in the evening I gave a sermon in the village Church on the words: "Thy lips, O, my spouse, drop as the honeycomb: honey and milk are under thy tongue; and the smell of thy garments is like the smell of Lebanon." Afterwards he remarked that the Word had touched him in an unusual way.

That night, after the service, we visited a home into which Death had entered. A prayer by a godly neighbour touched him deeply. It was that of the excellent Alexander MacFarquhar. The last Psalm sung at family worship ended with the words:—

> "And plenteous redemption
> Is ever found with Him,
> And from all his iniquities
> He Israel shall redeem."

From that night he was a different man, truly a new creation in Christ Jesus. Meantime, his health broke down, and for the rest of his life he alternated between bright spiritual hopes and deep anxieties. In the summer he accompanied his younger sister, Peggy, to the moor where the air was kinder and more wholesome. During that time he could not pass a flower without speaking of the loveliness of the One Who had "done all things well." But the old temptations to unbelief and doubt at times harassed him severely. Before he died a dark night descended on his spirit. His faith was almost totally eclipsed. But the Sun of Righteousness arose again on his soul with healing in His wings.

Shortly before the end he read in the daily press an account of one of the last public speeches of a national Churchman, who closed his earthly life by denying such doctrines as the Virgin Birth and the Resurrection from the dead. Satan used the foolish negations of this poor and graceless man by suggesting to him that men of learning would not believe what less educated men like himself accepted without reserve. But the Lord delivered him out of this snare in a way that was strange in his own eyes.

One night he felt as if someone stood beside his bed, and asked him to listen. Then he heard a voice of surpassing power and majesty. "In the beginning was the Word, and the Word was with God, and the Word was God." . . . . "Heaven and earth shall pass away, but My word shall not pass away . . . . " "For ever, O Lord, Thy word is settled in heaven." The enunciation of those great truths seemed to him to fill all space. He was then reminded that God's Word alone was supreme and eternal, while all other and contrary voices would finally die away and be silenced. On that early morning he took his Bible in his hands, and gave fervent thanks to God for having so solemnly, if so mysteriously, confirmed to him anew its truth and everlastingness. His mind, as usual, was cool and normal. To him the whole experience was very, very real and laden with comfort.

The Bible was his only comfort in his great sufferings. One day he said to me, "I have been drawing much consolation from those words, 'My peace I leave with you.' The more I draw from this life-giving spring the more the Lord puts into it for me." His last words on earth were: "Sweet now is the rest." These words he whispered into the ear of his kind and devoted wife.

In the following letter, written to a near relative after he got news of her conversion, he lifts the veil to let us see how the Lord had led him in his darker days.

> " Today has been one of the happiest in my life. When I read the last portion of your letter my heart grew big with joy, and my tears were of joy too. I think I know in some small measure the meaning of the Scripture which says: 'There is joy in the presence of the angels of God over one sinner that repenteth.' You ask me to remember you, but I cannot help you unless it is given me from the merciful God Himself. I will pray, however, that you will be led to see the preciousness of Christ. Oh, how dry my remarks look on paper, but were you to tell me that you inherited twenty millions in money it would, in my estimation, be no news worth repeating in comparison with a revelation of the love of Christ to your soul.
>
> Now do not despair if you be beset with terrible temptations that what you are striving for is self-conducted, and is the result of natural emotions. If we are really unsure

of ourselves it may be a healthy state to be in. The tempter would have us sometimes lie complacent, and be very sure of ourselves. Some of those who are still ruled by the world, the flesh, and Satan, are often self-righteous and sure of themselves.

Let me tell you what helped myself and strengthened me. I always — even in my darkest moments — tried to pray. That is our greatest privilege on earth — that we may, through Christ, communicate in secret with our Creator.

I used to pray like this: 'Oh, merciful God, I do not need to tell Thee my condition. Thou knowest my sins, and needs, my hardness, my ignorance. I realise I deserve to be for ever cast from Thy sight as a sinner, but for the sake of the Saviour Who came into this world to save sinners Put me "among the number," for His sake.'

I am simply giving you an idea of the way I trod before I tasted of His indescribable love. Latterly I could not even pray like that. I had really nothing — nothing to say, before an holy and just God. I would remain on my knees awaiting my doom. It was when I thought I was lost for ever that the VOICE came out of the storm: 'For He shall deliver the needy when he crieth; the poor also, and him that hath no helper.' (Psalm 72).

I hope and would fain believe that you also will hear and recognise that Voice. That will be the most wonderful moment in your life, and you will never get over the wonder of God's speaking a word of mercy to you, in this life or in the life to come.

For my part all things were new. Everything was holy and sweet for a time. Of you I can say that I never loved you as I love you now. Continue looking to God, and He will in no wise cast you out. Do not be indifferent in the matter of your salvation. Do not put Him away. The Spirit of God is kind and loving, but easily grieved.

Oh, to think that my ——— is now a King's daughter! I will conclude with the words my mother used to repeat, 'With men this is impossible; but with God all things are possible.' (Matthew 19)."

The departure of a brother beloved was a great grief to me, and here I may mention that these separations and bereavements coincided in my own life with another prolonged season of affliction. The Lord, however sustained and comforted me by His Word. One night He visited my soul in the words, "For this shall everyone that is godly pray unto Thee in a time when Thou mayest be found: surely in the floods of great waters they shall not come nigh unto him." (Psalm 32). A gleam of light and hope reached me also through the words of another Psalm: "Be of good courage and He shall strengthen your heart, all ye that hope in the Lord." (Psalm 31).

I recall how another measure of comfort reached me through a lovely and vivid dream. I dreamt that, in the company of others of God's people, I was going at a swift and tireless pace toward a beautiful country which we could see afar off. The glorious dawn of a new day was just touching the summit of the distant mountains. We went forward singing the words of Psalm 73:

"Thou, with thy counsel while I live
wilt me conduct and guide;
And to thy glory afterward
receive me to abide."

After some time I left with my beloved wife, who had so tenderly nursed me during my illness, to breathe the wholesome air of her native Strathpeffer. But my weakness and spiritual depression continued, so much so that more than once I contemplated giving up my work for a period.

Later in the year I went to Glenshiel where my friend, Mr Andrew Sutherland, the minister there, welcomed me to his home. From there I crossed over to my native Island. In the way a kindly providence led me into the company of a fellow minister, the much loved Mr Murdoch MacRae of Kinloch, Lewis. As this servant of the Lord began to relate some of his own spiritual and bodily sufferings and infirmities I came to realise that "the **same** afflictions are accomplished in our brethren who are in the world."

One early morning in our home in Lewis I awoke out of sleep with these words, "And to the angel of the Church in Philadelphia write . . . . " What the words meant I could not at first tell. With the dawn of day I read that wonderful letter written to the "angel," or messenger, of that Church. What a great letter that is! "I know thy works; behold, I have set before thee an open door, and no man can shut it . . . . for thou hast a little strength and hast kept My word, and hast not denied My Name." (Rev. 3) The exceeding great and precious promises in which this letter abounds I was afraid to grasp lest I should be guilty of presumption. On the other hand how perfectly did I see my own state mirrored in that tender phrase — "Thou hast a little strength." For many days afterwards I basked in the warm sunshine of this reassuring word, and prayed earnestly that such an inheritance as it holds forth to those who overcome might also be mine. The conviction now formed itself in my mind that weak as I was, the Lord would have me return to my work. Which thing, in fear and trembling, I did.

The hard lessons which I had to learn in this season of suffering were many. I learned, for example, that the power and malice of Satan are something of which we know but little. Who, indeed, can know wholly the "depths of Satan?" Let those be thankful who know not what is implied in God's mysterious permission to let some of His people fall into the "hand of the cruel," for however short the season. He knows how to exploit those seasons in our life when our strength is reduced, and when we may fail to employ every weapon and every protective grace of God's spiritual armoury.

The tender pity and the love of God were also revealed to me in a new, or in a more tender, way. Truly, in the words of the Psalmist, He made all my bed for me in the day of trouble. If many of His people are in His hospital here, He is also the One Who nurses them tenderly. It is in our affliction that we discover the depth of sympathy, compassion and love which is in His heart toward us. When, like an ailing child, I stretched out my hands towards Him, He carried me in His arms. Under His wings I found healing, and in His word I found a balm. "In all their afflictions He was afflicted, and the angel of His presence saved them." (Is. 63). My deep affection for these words I can trace back to a time when they touched my soul with a pathos and tenderness such as I have seldom, if ever, felt in this world. It was as if the words came from the very heart of Him who pities us as a father pities his children, and who is ever touched with a feeling of our infirmity.

A quickened sympathy for the suffering people of God was, I hope, another effect of this experience. How little we know of what some of God's people have to suffer in this life! There is sometimes at the heart of Christian experience a deep inarticulate pain which may lie beyond the ken of many Christian people and ministers. God sees fit to give some of His people a share of the unwanted cup which their fellow believers must drink. This He does, as in the case of Paul, that they might be able to comfort them with the comfort wherewith they themselves are comforted of God. (II Cor. 1).

One evening, for example, at one of our weekly meetings of prayer, I mentioned some of the trials to which many of the Lord's people were often subjected. That night, and before I reached my home, three persons separately joined me in the way to thank me for touching in my sermon on fears and temptations which they thought had afflicted none but themselves. In a strange way they were happy in knowing that others were also passing through these same dark vales.

And one would wish to assure the tried people of God that in His keeping there is nothing to fear. In many cases it will take more than time to prove that God is wise and loving in what He allows. In the higher sphere of His grace He gives His people night and day. "Weeping may endure for a night, but joy cometh in the morning." (Ps. 30). This was the discovery of Hezekiah of old who came to know that his night of trial came only to bless him and bearing many choice gifts under its dark robe. "O Lord, by these things men live, and in all these things is the life of my spirit; so wilt Thou recover me and make me to live." (Is. 38).

A more lasting and fruitful benefit has been an ever-growing dependence on God in His grace and Word. God, wrapped up in His Own eternal happiness and sufficiency, could have done without **us**, but every moment in life the broken in heart consciously need **His** help. He sends us pain and weakness that we might learn how to lean on the Beloved. He permits the enemy to buffet us that we may resort to His strong Name as our daily refuge. And how wonderful it is to know that He whose abode is the high and holy place, loves as much to dwell with the poor man or woman groaning in the tabernacle of clay as among the vast glories and the unceasing praises of the Heavenly world!

Though I have been guided into somewhat calmer waters since that day, the world has taken on a different colour. It appears more remote and more empty. As, I humbly hope, the Eternal Home comes more into view one ceases to regret having to take an everlasting farewell of this broken and shadowed life. We would, on the other hand, tarry here for a while that we might do something for the One whose love and labour we can never repay.

Though I stayed in Glasgow for a while during this season of weakness, the conviction now settled on my mind that after seventeen years in Glasgow the time had come when I should leave the city for an easier sphere of labour. In prayer I asked the Lord if I had not "tarried long enough on this mountain?" The burden of ministering to a city congregation was so heavy that I could not now bear it without a long period of comparative rest. The Lord heard my prayer and allowed my plea. One early morning, the Lord, by the following words, awoke me out of sleep. "God hath spoken in His holiness. I will rejoice, I will divide Shechem, and mete out the valley of Succoth." Not long afterwards letters reached me from several congregations inviting me to become their pastor. One of these which was from the congregation of Resolis in Ross-shire. I was led to accept.

CHAPTER TEN

GLASGOW DAYS

NOW THAT I was on the eve of leaving Glasgow sorrow filled my heart. Would I ever again in this life enjoy such a blessing as I did in my congregation there and among a people many of whom truly feared the Lord?

There was a good Christian woman in the congregation who took me aside one day. She whispered words of comfort into my soul. "I pray for you always," she said, "and the other morning you were given to me in these words: 'And he that reapeth receiveth wages, and gathereth fruit to life eternal; that both he that soweth and he that reapeth may rejoice together.' You are going to leave us, but the Lord will continue to sustain you in your work."

My last Communion in Glasgow was to me both solemn and memorable. Mr Ranald Fraser, then minister at Lochcarron, ended the Sabbath service in much spiritual comfort. During the prayer which followed the sermon, as he asked the Lord to honour us with His presence at His supper, a sense of awe seemed to pervade the minds of many present. Some were quite melted down under the felt blessing. To me personally God's presence was so real that I was sure that as soon as I opened my eyes I would see the attendant angels "who desire to look into" the symbols of Christ's love and sufferings. "Lord, it is good for us to be here," were words which some present would have uttered; but we have here, on the other hand, but the "tabernacle of a wayfaring man."

We parted from the Glasgow Congregation in the bonds of Christian tenderness. On the words: 'But the God of all grace Who hath called us unto His eternal glory by Christ Jesus, after that ye have suffered a while, make you perfect, stablish, strengthen, settle you,' I based my farwell sermon. And in heaven I hope to see not a few of those whom I left that Sabbath evening, some of whom I was to meet no more in time.

Before I bring these reminiscences of our years in Glasgow to an end, I should like to make mention of some dear friends who no longer inhabit this lower vale. Our Glasgow Presbytery, which is the largest in the Church, was made up of men who were truly the excellent of the earth. One of these was my near-neighbour in Partick. This was the Rev. Alexander MacLeod, minister of Crow Road Free Church. Mr MacLeod was a native of Scourie, in Sutherland. For twelve years we lived and laboured in the bonds of brotherly affection, and no situation, such as is bound to arise sometimes in congregations of close proximity, was allowed to mar or cool our friendship. An able and exercised Christian man, he knew both the conflicts which are peculiar to the Christian life, and the consolations of God. In all our personal difficulties we were often led to help one another — the one strengthening the other as the Lord would have us do. To part company with this beloved brother was a sore wrench. His coming to Nairn a few years after my own translation to Resolis made me very happy. Mr MacLeod suddenly died while on a visit to Palestine in the Spring of 1965, greatly mourned by all who knew him.

Another devoted friend was the Rev. Andrew Sutherland, of Duke Street Church — to whom I have already referred. A native of Dornoch, Mr Sutherland had, in his younger days, the inestimable privilege of being in touch with a generation of Christian men and women noted for their spiritual discernment and nearness to the Lord. In his early days such men as David Ross, James Matheson and Angus Murray were still on the scene. Although he looked on James Matheson as a man whose prophetic insight and prayerful life commanded the deep respect of all who knew him, his affections went out to Angus Murray in a special way.

Mr Sutherland was, indeed, but a mere lad when God visited him in a day of His power; and the brook which ran near his home could testify to his long and earnest pleadings with the Angel of the Covenant. The fragrant breath of prayer remained, indeed, in his soul all his days. Throughout the years it was no unusual thing for members of his family to hear his voice in the night seasons at the throne of Grace. The rousing appeals and solemn warnings which characterised his preaching from the beginning of his ministry, the Lord, we believe, often blessed in the conversion of souls. I vividly remember one of these moving sermons based on the words, 'Come in, thou blessed of the Lord, wherefore standest thou without.' The large congregation who listened that evening to his message were earnestly entreated, by the aid of God's Spirit, to receive the Prince of Life into their hearts. It was a characteristic sermon. One could not but feel the depth of pity and love for perishing souls which lay behind his words. Also, as a comforter of God's suffering people, Mr Sutherland had few equals. He knew their trials, and he also knew how to speak 'a word in season' to their weary hearts.

In Glasgow he laboured for twenty years. The large, appreciative congregation which waited on his ministry there, brought all his gifts and graces into activity. His pastoral sympathy made him a much-loved friend in the many homes which he regularly visited throughout the city. The link between him and many of his Glasgow friends remained unbroken to the end.

All his ministerial life Mr Sutherland suffered from total deafness. But his inability to converse with his friends brought him nearer to the One whose Presence and Word he so much enjoyed. One day, for example, a friend walked into his room unobserved and unheard, and such was his obvious enjoyment of God's presence in secret prayer that his friend afterwards spoke about it in public as an instance of how God's saints walk with Him by faith and personal communion. One of his last sermons made it clear that all his desire was already in heaven with Christ. His theme was the blessed and precious hope of seeing the King in His beauty, and the land of far distances. When, in the Spring of 1963, I stood by the grave of my friend, in Fodderty, Ross-shire, I could not but long for the happy day when we would meet again.

During my Glasgow ministry we had a visit in our church from the minister of my boyhood days (to whom I have already referred), the Rev. Duncan MacDougall. Mr

MacDougall had just returned from the Canadian field. His sermon that evening on "the glory of Lebanon, and the excellency of Carmel and Sharon" was laden with beauty and life, and made a deep impression on the congregation.

During his ministry at Ness, in Lewis, Mr MacDougall once preached a remarkable sermon on the words: "He sware by him who liveth for ever and ever that there should be time no longer." (Rev. 10). On that occasion he spoke of Heaven as the place from which all the criteria or standards by which we measure time here are absent. Heaven is an Eternal Day — "for there is no night there." Here we measure the day by the rising and the setting of the sun, but in Heaven our sun shall no more go down. That country has no need of the sun, "for the Lamb is the light thereof." In Heaven we neither hunger nor thirst. The physical phases through which we pass here are unknown there. There no one dies and none is born. Age never wearies, for all have the plenitude of eternal life. Heaven is a continuous state of bliss, where one day with the Lord is as a thousand years and where we go on making ever fresh and ever joyous discoveries of God's glory and of "the unsearchable riches of Christ." When Mr MacDougall had finished his sermon on that New Year's Day his aged friend and assistant came forward and thanked him for a profound word which had brought them to the portals of the Eternal City "that hath foundations and whose builder and maker is God." Mr MacDougall passed to his eternal rest not long after his last visit to our home.

Another friend, Mr A. MacLeod, who laboured in those days in the Govan congregation, was also a man who exercised an active and profitable ministry. A deeply experimental preacher, he knew how to comfort those of God's people who were cast down. When he enjoyed the freedom of the Spirit his sermons could be both moving and edifying. On several occasions I listened to Mr MacLeod in our Church in Glasgow. Two of his sermons I can still remember. They were based on the words: "Ye have tarried long enough on this mount," and, "Come with me from Lebanon my sister, my spouse." Seldom did I enjoy in public so much of God's presence as I did listening to his exhortations to maintain a closer walk with God by a greater spiritual detachment from things seen.

This worthy man I saw in his last illness. By that time he had returned to his native island to minister in the congregation of Back. As I moved away from his bed — never to see him again in this world — I quoted the words: "But I shall see you again and our hearts shall rejoice; and your joy no man shall take from you." Which, when I did, he smiled and waved his hand in a final farewell in this world.

In our Glasgow Congregation we had three meetings of prayer every week. To listen to the good men who 'called on the name of the Lord' was a privilege the value of which I came to realise more fully when I left it. Many a time I would fain have sat for ever in that place, so real was God's presence among us. There, indeed, I often had a Bethel on earth.

There was one memorable night, shortly before I left Glasgow, when I was reminded in a way that I cannot describe, that I would never again, in the public means of grace, enjoy the blessing of those days. The tears which I shed that night were truly a sad foretaste of the spiritual decline which I came to know so well in after-years in other parts of the land where the Lord had become a stranger. In such places it was not easy to sing the Lord's song.

My elders in the Session were truly men of God. They were not learned, but they had the knowledge of the holy. They were men devoted to God's Cause and to the Church which they served. By their loyalty and zeal they proved themselves to be pillars in God's temple.

Sometimes in Glasgow, on entering the homes of the rich, I found that the true lady was not always in the drawing-room but in the kitchen. Spiritual refinement springs from God's grace in the heart, and not from the superficial fashion of this world. And the old truth is ever new: 'not many mighty, not many noble, are called.' The 'servants' who moved about in the halls of Caesar were the 'saints,' while the Emperor and his circle of admirers knew not the Lord.

One of the terrible ironies of that solemn day awaiting mankind, will be the reversal of all human categories. 'The first shall be last, and the last shall be first.'

In reading the Gospel one is impressed by the fact that although our Lord's forerunner, John the Baptist, was slain by an evil woman, no woman ever lifted her voice against Himself but to bless Him, nor her hand but to minister to Him. Those who labour in the Gospel must often echo the thanksgiving of Paul in his deep appreciation of feminine service. 'I commend unto you Phoebe our sister who is a servant of the Church . . . . Greet Mary, who bestowed much labour on us.' Of the many elect ladies who graced our congregations in Glasgow, I can only mention a few.

One of these was an excellent Christian woman from Kilchoan in Argyll. Mrs Gray — for that was her name — lived very near the Lord, and, in her latter years, her desire to be with Christ continued to deepen, till she came at last to the land of her desire.

She was a lady of spiritual weight and discernment. While health remained her presence with her devoted daughter in the Church brought its own blessing.

There was another elderly 'mother in Israel' whose fellowship I sometimes enjoyed. Mrs Grant, who lived in Bishopbriggs, was a native of Brora in Sutherland. In her younger days she had been in touch with some of the eminent men and women of God for which the North was once famous. The spiritual flavour of her early associations she retained to the end. My occasional visits to her home were moments of spiritual refreshing. In her own words, she would not care to begin the day without the Lord giving her a token of His love. Living alone, she must have, perhaps unconsciously formed the habit of addressing the Lord as if He were beside her — as He truly was — in her room. Once, as I sat in her drawing-room, I could hear her affectionate and adoring exclamations as she moved about in her little kitchen preparing our cup of tea. The Lord's Presence filled her heart and her home, while at the same time she became increasingly conscious of the plague of her heart. When this 'jewel' was given its setting in her Lord's crown above, the tiny church where she worshipped on earth could not but miss her presence and prayers.

There was another choice Christian woman in our congregation on whom I called in her last illness. She shared the home with a devoted husband and daughter. But since they were strangers to God they were quite out of sympathy with her spiritual exercises and enjoyments. After I had engaged in prayer at her bedside she asked me if I saw "the others" in the room. When I enquired whether she meant her daughter and husband she said: "O, not them; but those others who have been here with me for many hours." I told her that what she saw I could only feel through the presence of the Lord which was truly there. She was entering the heavenly Canaan, and her pilgrimage was now over. Unlike her, I had not yet come to the place where the veil of our mortal life here is taken off our eyes. "The others" remained with her to the end. They had come to accompany her to her eternal Home. In her conversation she was perfectly rational — resting in the deep calm of God's presence.

In those early days there was another good woman in our congregation by whose Christian conversation I was often refreshed. She belonged to an older generation of Christians. Her name was Mary Smith, a native of Lewis. Mary's devotion to God and His house was deep and sincere. On leaving the church on the Sabbath evening she would sometimes remark to a friend, "Another Sabbath is gone, but Thursday will soon be here." On the Thursday night she would be back again at the weekly prayer meeting. To her the tabernacles of God were truly amiable. She told me once of a Sabbath evening in Glasgow when she went to hear one of the visiting ministers who was assisting at a Communion. He was the excellent Mr John Macdonald of Sleat, in the Isle of Skye. She had never seen nor heard him before. His sermon that evening was based on the words: "As the beast (or herd) goeth down into the valley so the Spirit of the Lord caused him to rest." For her the sermon was bathed in power and spiritual consolation. Her cup of blessing that night God filled to overflowing. She was quite enraptured in her soul. The deep impression which that message made on her spirit remained with her to the end. It was, to her, a foretaste of the pleasures which are for evermore at God's right hand. When God took this gracious woman to Himself we could not but miss her presence and prayers in the means of grace.

A friend of Mary Smith, who worked as a housekeeper in Glasgow, once told me of a day when for the first time she met my father in a certain home in the city. The Communion season was observed in our Glasgow congregation at the time. This lady expressed her keen disappointment that, because of other unavoidable duties, she could not be present at the evening service at which one of her favourite ministers — Mr William Cameron of Resolis — was to preach. Her master's dinner hour, she explained, coincided with the hour of the service. My father, observing her sorrow of heart, said to her: "If that is how you feel, the Lord, I believe, will enable you to attend His house to-night." "I am afraid," she said, "that will be impossible, for my master, at the moment, is alone." When, however, she reached her place of residence a note was awaiting her to say that he was having dinner out with friends, and that the rest of the day could be all her own. By this incident the Lord enabled her to know again that He is the hearer of prayer and that his secret is often with those who fear Him.

Before I left Glasgow I had become acutely aware of how the tide of spiritual life had ebbed — more manifestly in those places where the Lord had once done 'many mighty works.' Once, for example, I was asked to conduct services in one of the nearer South-Western Isles where we had a few small congregations. This once-favoured isle was, over a century ago, the scene of a fruitful evangelical revival. Now it had almost become a mere holiday resort. In a letter I was directed to a boarding-house where, unknown and unwelcomed, I ate my morsel alone. Later in the day I addressed a few elderly people who appeared at the servce. Afterwards I found my way to a seaside seat where I waited some time for a conveyance that would take me several miles to a house where I could rest for the night. That day as I watched the crowds in search of their fleeting joys, and as I saw the residential terraces with "no room" anywhere for one who was trying to serve the Lord, I became strangely aware of what I knew before — of being an unwanted stranger on the earth. But the joy produced by this reflection I would not part with for anything which this world could bestow.

On a Communion Sabbath in another remote Congregation my mind was so grieved over the sad state of the Cause of

Christ that on the following night I paced the floor of my bedroom in deep concern. Before dawn, however, the Lord composed my spirit in the words of the dying king: 'Although mine house be not so with God, yet hath He made with me an everlasting covenant ordered in all things and sure; for this is all my salvation, and all my desire, although He maketh it not to grow' (2 Samuel 23). But let me end with the words, "Fear not, O land, be glad and rejoice; for the Lord will do great things" (Job 2 v. 21).

Chapter Eleven

RESOLIS

MY SETTLEMENT in Resolis took place in the summer of 1951. This historic and once-favoured Ross-shire parish was, over a century ago, a garden of the Lord. Such names as that of Mr Hector MacPhail, Mr Donald Sage, Mr John MacIver and Mr William Cameron were associated with the evangelical revival and tradition which made this corner of Highlands so famous. The saving truths of free grace which those and other men preached gave birth to that pure and primitive form of Christian life of which one reads in the New Testament, and which sometimes since then appeared in those places where the Bible was supreme and on which the Spirit was poured out.

Mr Cameron — as well as his excellent family — I knew personally. He was a man who united great gifts of mind and heart to much grace and lowliness of life. In the pulpit he was dependent on the aid of the Spirit, and on the sympathy and prayers of the hearers, to give effect and elevation to his message. When he enjoyed spiritual freedom he would touch heights of evangelic eloquence and devotional warmth which few in his generation could reach. At such times the ease and power with which he proclaimed the glad tidings marked his efforts as the genuine fruit of the Spirit of God. When this freedom was denied he could only drag his sermon haltingly to its close.

In the North, and especially in Easter Ross, one could not but observe that where the Lord had once reaped a great harvest the land was now almost spiritually barren. But there were still here and there among the people those who were "as the shaking of the olive tree and as the gleaning grapes when the vintage is done." (Is. 24). The moral tone of the community, however, remained on a high level. The people were strictly honest, kindly and respectable. The drunkard, the Sabbath breaker, the swearer, and the thief were rare specimens. And this was something which could not be said of many other places in our day.

When my predecessor, Mr Cameron, came to Resolis, there was still on the scene quite a cluster of men and women who carried the spiritual flavour of other days. One of those men once informed him that as a lad on the way to Church he could, on occasions, overhear the subdued voices of men and women in prayer behind walls, hedges and trees. "The voice of the turtle" was still heard in the land. The afterglow from "the days of open vision" had not yet quite faded. When I came on the scene the older generation of Christians had nearly all passed away. As in other places once highly favoured, many of the people were being caught up in an accelerated process of materialism. The minds of many were being drawn away from the old ways through the material inducements of the times, and through the dangerous and distracting sources of entertainment of a new age. One feared that it was the old story of the people "waxing fat" in temporal things, but undergoing an unconscious impoverishment in the realm of the spirit. The few who had escaped the deadening influences of a different age were, however, and by contrast, shining lights in the darkness of the times.

One or two of these are deserving of mention. When I came to Resolis my senior elder was John McFarquhar of Cullicudden. This worthy man loved the Lord. God's Word was his constant meditation. John once told me that he was one day sitting alone in his home thinking over a certain aspect of God's dealings with his people in his providence. He found the subject a great deep. That day someone seemed to stand behind him and to say: "It is not for you to be thinking of such things." The sinister whisper greatly disturbed him. On the Sabbath morning however, as he was walking into the church, Mr Cameron was giving out the opening words of a Psalm which reads:

"The whole works of the Lord our God
Are great above all measure,
Sought out they are of every one
That doth therein take pleasure." (Psalm 111).

"Then," said John, "it was my turn to say to the Devil, 'And where are you now in the face of God's holy Word?' "

John knew the way to the Throne of Grace. In prayer he often made mention of the promised glory of the latter days. He longed for the blessed age when the knowledge of the Lord shall cover the earth as the waters cover the deep. There was a wonderful hour in his life when, on the mountain-top of communion with God, he was favoured with a glimpse of that age of Gospel peace awaiting the Church in the future. By faith he saw the good land from his Pisgah. He died a happy man, assured that his Portion and Treasure was in Heaven.

A younger man than John was Robert Grigor of Springfield. Robert was no longer a young man when he came to know the Good Part. His growth in grace, however, was so rapid, and his growing affection for God, His people and His House was so marked, that it was obvious to his friends that the Lord was preparing him for an unfading inheritance above. The day he died I happened to be looking through a window in the Manse toward his home at Springfield. All of a sudden I found these words in my mind:

> "And of the place where once it was
> It shall no more be known." (Psalm 103).

The conviction was so strong in my mind that our friend was going away that I turned to my wife and said: "Robert Grigor is soon leaving us." That evening he passed away. We had called on him a few days before he died. "Satan and sin," he said, "would keep me in their grasp; but Christ will deliver me, for He has an hold of me." These words expressed his great hope as he was about to enter the eternal world.

With the passing of these men, a Church Session which had been in existence for several generations, and which was noted for its charity, wisdom and piety, came almost to the point of extinction.

A few days before I settled in Resolis the Lord visited me in those endearing words of Psalm 23 — "He maketh me to lie down in green pastures; he leadeth me beside the still waters." I was disposed to give these words a remote and spiritual application, but when on a perfect summer day we reached the Resolis Manse, with its nearby meadows and garden, beyond the wall of which a clean stream flowed softly, I saw the perfect and literal fulfilment of the promise. Looking across the lovely valley where the manse is situated, and beholding the distant western hills clad in a dreamy blue haze, I could not help thinking, 'This is that valley of Succoth of which the Lord had spoken to me a year ago.'

There was in Resolis, as in Glenmoriston, a quiet and even pathway near our house where I could, under the cover of night, commune at times with the Lord. There were times when, sitting at home, I thought I could feel the touch of an unseen Hand upon my spirit, leading me to my trysting-place with the unseen Angel of the Covenant. Those, in retrospect, are treasured memories. How often did I look up at the night sky rejoicing with all the people of God in the words, "He telleth the number of the stars; he calleth them all by their names . . . . The Lord taketh pleasure in them that fear Him, in those who hope in His mercy." (Psalm 147).

But, on the other hand, a painful pre-occupation of those days was the attempt to review my life and work in God's vineyard. This exercise of mind often filled me with much sorrow. The years were swiftly receding and I felt I had done but little for Him who had done so much for me. There were also sad moments when I recalled the early days in Greenock, Strachur and Glenmoriston. With another I could say:

> "Where is the blessedness I knew
> when first I saw the Lord?
> Where is the soul-refreshing view
> of Jesus and His Word?
>
> Return, O, Holy Dove, return!
> Sweet messenger of rest!
> I hate the sins which made Thee mourn,
> and drove Thee from my breast."

Life in retrospect is, indeed, made up of sunshine and cloud. Looking back on the years that are gone, I can say with Jacob that "few and evil have been the days of my life." And no one whose conscience is in any way tender and whose memory of other days remains clear, can escape from some measure of the shadow of regret. "The years which the locusts have eaten," are sad words. There are regrets over things done and things left undone. One looks back on privileges misused and precious time misspent. The many hours during which one might have wrestled with the Lord in prayer or have been engaged in some spiritual and worthwhile task, have often unconsciously slipped away. The sin of omission is very grievous. And what of our many lapses in thoughts, words and deeds, which, like shadows, so often darken our spirits? How easy it is to speak of our peculiarities or dispositional infirmities, when we should really speak of "the sin that doth so easily beset us." But opposite the mountains of our sin is the two-fold promise: "The blood of Jesus Christ His Son cleanseth us from all sin." "Who is a God like unto Thee, that pardoneth iniquity and passeth by the transgressions of the remnant of thine heritage? He retaineth not his anger for ever because he delighteth in mercy." "And He who hath begun the good work in you shall perform it till the Day of Jesus Christ." On these words and promises, like a nail fastened in a sure place, we should pin all our hope before God.

The daily warfare with a sinful nature is a story which most Christians could tell. The imperative word, "Walk thou before me and be thou perfect," the people of God would obey if they could. Some mornings I would awake and say, "I shall be wise and sin no more," but the night would find me mourning over the transgressions of the day. How often did I try to "bury" my sinful self for ever in a grave! There were deceptive hours when I thought I had succeeded in doing this; but I knew but little of the deceitfulness of sin. Books and sermons on the life of 'Constant Victory' and 'Entire Consecration' I would read, only to lapse into a state of sorrow since others appeared to attain to a spiritual standard unknown to me. Every attempt to put off the old man of sin made me realise my own helplessness. This, my sorest cross, I cannot hope to lay down till I leave this tabernacle "wherein we groan being burdened."

During my years in Resolis my greatest source of consolation was that the Lord followed me there with the joyful sound of His Word. My soul, as He was wont, He continued to visit in the night. (Ps. 17). When the enemy began to rub salt into my old sores His ever-seasonable words proved an healing balm. One of the clusters of truth which stayed me then was that of the third Psalm. "Many there be that say to my soul, there is no help for him in God. But Thou, O Lord, art a shield for me; my glory and the lifter up of my head." On the Sabbath morning in which these words were let fall into my mind, I was so uplifted in my affections and desire that I was comforted to know that the only barrier between me and the "everlasting rest" was the breath which moved in my body.

In Resolis I was often spiritually refreshed by my visits to several homes there. Of these I can only mention a few. The three excellent ladies who lived in those days at Upper Springfield always welcomed me at their door. Their conversation seldom deviated from the great things of God's Word and His unfailing mercy toward those who fear Him. "Anna" was the listener whose eyes unvariably filled as God's Word touched her heart, while Mary delighted in recalling past days and old friends in the Lord who had meantime "fallen asleep." Older in years but younger in the faith was Christina. Her own spiritual conversion at a late hour was the greatest event in her life. Although two of these Christian ladies did not belong to my own church their presence in our services — while their strength remained — was always an encouragement, for I knew that they remembered me at the Throne of Grace.

Another gracious lady was Catherine MacRae who lived at Balblair. Catherine, who was the eldest member in our congregation, was one of the most sincere and affectionate women I ever knew. To visit her home was to experience an outburst of joy, which, somehow, she could not control. Her inward desire after a greater degree of assurance of God's love she often expressed in words which, unknown to herself, made it clear that God's love truly lodged in her heart. Never did I sit on her hearth but I felt I was in the presence of one in whose heart the Lord had His abode.

Another person whose conversation I sometimes enjoyed was a man locally known as "old Mr Whyte" who lived at the Bog of Resolis. Almost totally deaf, he invariably began the bedside talk himself, and seldom did it touch on anything on the natural or local level. Whenever the Name, the glory or the work of the Redeemer were mentioned his eyes would fill, and his lips would move in silent prayer and praise. Nearly a hundred years old, he would speak with deep apprehension of the terrifying changes which had come over the world in his lifetime, often bringing his remarks to a close with the words, "Oh, man, we are living in fearful days."

There was another man who during my years in Resolis, proved himself to be a pillar in the temple of God. He was Mr William MacKenzie of Drumdyre. It was in his public prayers that one truly felt the depth of piety which dwelt in his heart. His public devotions were, as a rule, brief, solemn and refreshing. His life of devotion to Christ he shared with his equally pious wife.

In our neighbouring congregation of Fortrose there were two or three families who, throughout my earlier years at Resolis, never failed to attend our evening services on alternate Sabbaths when no service was held in their own church. When these appeared at our meetings accompanied by their families one could always be sure of a measure of spiritual freedom. Their interest in the Good Tidings was often a rebuke to those who, living in sight of God's house, spent the Lord's Day in their homes, lying in the thick folds of spiritual death, and deeply buried in their earthly concerns. But this is just what the Lord has said. "I will take you one of a city and two of a family and bring you to Zion." But my friendship with those jewels of grace often proved refreshing to my spirit.

During my latter years in Resolis, I was happy in having as my neighbour in the Parish Church, a man who was faithful to the eternal verities of God's Word. The Rev. John Newall — who was my younger College contemporary and whom I mentioned before — was a native of Lewis. A man of gentle disposition, circumspect in walk, and of sound theological grasp, he could not but command — as he did — the respect and affection of God's people in the community. Preaching on alternate Sabbaths on the outskirts of the parish, and sometimes to the same people, I knew that my doctrine would always coincide with his.

One of my most memorable hours in Resolis was on a certain evening early in 1966. That evening I sat down to write a letter to a ministerial friend. In wishing him "the blessing of the Lord," during the coming days I quoted the words of Moses which speak of "the good will of him who dwelt in the bush." I had hardly penned these words than I felt an overpowering sense of God's presence touching my spirit. It was, as at other times, as if something unspeakably sweet and solemn had suddenly, if very gently, invaded the whole of my inward life. Leaving the room where I sat I entered another apartment where I could be alone. But my peace and enjoyment were still so overpowering that, after a while, I went outside, where I walked in front of our church and where — if that were possible — my awareness of God's presence seemed to deepen. What was uppermost in my heart that evening was the desire to praise God, and a longing for the day when, in the great congregation above, I would be able to offer Him perfect praise. "Praise **waiteth** for thee, O God, in Sion." (Ps. 65). A few nights before then I had been reading in a book that the word "waiteth" in this Psalm conveys the idea of the deep inexpressible desire within the gracious soul to praise God. It is, to repeat an illustration, like the outstretched neck of a little bird in its nest. The instinct to fly and to sing is there, but not until it reaches full maturity can it have its perfect exercise, or can it soar with its own kind to warble its song in the sky! That evening I seemed to be in close communion with those who were already within the veil with Christ — some of whom I have known and loved in this world. That night also, and before I closed my eyes in sleep, I could not but thank the Lord for this much needed drink which refreshed my weary soul. That God was present in this, to me, wonderful visitation He confirmed by His awakening me out of sleep in the early morning with these words, "Whom have I in the heavens but thee, and there is none on earth that I desire beside thee." These tastes or glimpses of "the Beloved" are precious beyond words. They make us long for the day when He shall no more vanish out of sight, but when we shall see Him as He is, and where He is. In that day He shall no more be as a wayfaring man "that turneth aside to tarry for a night."

Some time after this I was again favoured with much nearness to the Lord in secret. I could not but praise Him for His everlasting unchangeableness, not only in His being, but in His love, His Covenant faithfulness, and in His promise. The eternal I AM, was, I felt, all the desire of my soul above and beyond all others both in Heaven and on earth. I felt also my love going out, in a way that I could not describe, to all who loved Him, both angels and men. But soon my prosperous state was turned into misery. Fiery darts from the bow of Satan began to pierce through my soul. These took the form of evil thoughts which reflected on the glory of God and which greatly distressed my mind. Although I knew they were not my thoughts, that they were utterly repugnant to my mind, and that I would have given a million worlds to be rid of them for ever and ever, yet I could not dissociate them from myself. But in those great depths, the Lord was my Helper. His word upheld me. Several nights in succession I awoke out of sleep with His word again in my mouth. "The Lord liveth, and blessed be my rock; and let the God of my salvation be exalted." (Ps. 18). "For this God is our God for ever and ever: he will be our guide even unto death." (Ps. 48). "My meditation of him shall be sweet; I will be glad in the Lord." (Ps. 104). Truly these words from the very lips of the Brother born for adversity, not only sweetened the waters of Marah, but they were also my shield in the hour of conflict with the great adversary.

About this time also I passed through another very solemn experience. It happened on a certain night as I was standing outside our manse door. All of a sudden, and as I was quietly repeating to myself the words of Psalm 90, a deep sense of God's presence, and the awe of His Being, took possession of my soul. The words were: "From everlasting to everlasting Thou art God. For a thousand years in Thy sight are but as yesterday when it is past, and as a watch in the night." There I stood still with my head bowed. Time was like something which had ceased to be. I felt like one whose existence was in the eternal present, where the unchangeable and for ever adorable God, was the only Reality. All the events and all the inhabitants of time, from its beginning to the end, had, I felt, faded out like a mere dream, or passed away as a tale that is told. The irrelevance and transitoriness of all created things impressed my spirit beyond what I could describe. God alone was "the all and in all." I knew that He was the blissful and eternal Home of all who love Him. That night, and as I walked abroad for a while, I felt I knew in a measure the meaning of the words which say that a thousand years with the Lord are but as one day and one day as a thousand years.

On subsequent occasions, when I visited this lovely and much loved corner of Ross-shire I could not but bless the the Lord for those seasons of communion with Him throughout the years I was there. I could not but agree with a Godly minister who at the end of a refreshing Communion season, quoted the words "The Lord is there." Because of the state of my health, we left Resolis in November 1968 to settle in Inverness. It was, indeed, a sore wrench to separate from our friends in that quiet pastoral corner of Ross-shire. A day or two before we left I was sustained and much affected by God visiting me in His promise. It was a reassuring word which He has given to His people in every age.

> "O God, what time Thou didst go forth
> before Thy people's face . . . . "

But here we have no continuing city; but blessed are they who are seeking the city which all the redeemed desire and for which God is preparing them.

Chapter Twelve

"THE WORD OF EXHORTATION"

AS THE YEARS roll on one comes to realise that the preaching of the Gospel is a work of faith. We try to sow the good seed in the hope that God may give it the increase. There are seasons when some of God's servants get discouraged; for although they sow prayerfully and often in tears, theirs is not the joy of harvest. In eternity however, they shall discover that their labour was not in vain, and that, unknown to themselves, the Word had taken deep root in some hearts. "Their works shall follow them." We knew of men who, in the Spring of the year, had carefully cultivated the soil and sown the seed but who, in the time of harvest, were no longer here. Others had reaped where they had sown. "Herein is a true saying, One soweth and another reapeth." And in the higher realm of grace the work goes on while some of the labourers are gathered Home.

It is good to remember also that in the Christian Church there are varieties of ministries. To some it is given to comfort, edify and nourish the people of God. Through the preaching of the Word they feed Christ's sheep and lambs. Others God honours particularly in the awakening of sinners. There are 'sons of thunder' whose words, by God's blessing, cause the dead to stir in their graves. And there is also the awesome ministry of judgment. God's mighty prophet was sent to a people whose word was ordained to harden their hearts. Have we not often seen how when, over the years, men and women sit under the sound of the Gospel, giving no response to the overtures of God's grace, their hearts harden, and their ears become dull? They listen, but they do not hear. They pine away in a state of deep spiritual unconcern while God's goodness passes by. Confronted with such persistent spiritual indifference many prophets and faithful men have wept in this world. Our Lord Himself tasted the bitterness of this when He wept over Jerusalem.

There is another ministry which, by the blessing of God, many have found surprisingly effectual. It is what one may call the ministry of the casual word. This is a way of approach to our fellow men which calls for sympathy, prayerfulness, affection and earnestness. To me it has sometimes been a source of wonder how God can bless the simple, unpremeditated word in the conversion of a soul, while one's more studied pulpit efforts may be sometimes barren of lasting results. Let me give one or two instances of this. I do this, especially, to encourage those who by their witness and prayers may be seeking to bring souls to Christ, and to show that "the God of all grace" may use the poorest of instruments to this end.

The first instance that I would mention is associated with a railway journey. In the compartment were two women, one of whom I did not know, but who was a near relative of an eminently godly woman. I quietly reminded this person of her spiritual background and the danger of forfeiting, through neglect or unbelief, such a great heritage as was hers. Some time afterwards her companion began to attend our prayer meetings. Although my remarks were not specifically directed to her, the words which I addressed to her friend had, I believe, sunk with saving power into her heart.

I recall another somewhat similar instance of the power of the brief spoken word. In a certain congregation I was invited to a home after a Church service. In saying farewell to a member of this family I said: "See that you keep on remembering that you have a never-dying soul which needs salvation." This remark, like a nail fastened in a sure place, God blessed to her salvation. From that hour she proved herself to be a consistent follower of the Lord, and a seeker of "a better country."

During one of my journeys in the North a friend once asked me to speak to a young man who stood a little behind us in a crowd outside a Church. It so happened that this man, whom I did not then recognise, was present at a marriage which I had conducted in one of our cities. In addressing the marriage party, I spoke of the everlasting covenant between the Lord and His Church, and how death would, sooner or later, dissolve every other tie. The piercing conviction that he was a stranger to the covenant love of God made this young man think seriously. From that hour he began to seek the Lord. Intelligent, and balanced in his outlook and judgment, he afterwards became a most useful and diligent officer-bearer in the Church of Christ. Truly, 'the wind bloweth where it listeth.'

There are some who are not far from the Kingdom of God. For various reasons they linger in the valley of decision. They long for someone to lead them, and who might help them to overcome the peculiar and personal difficulties in the way. Once I was led to speak to an elderly lady in Ross-shire who seemed to be somewhat confused in her spiritual outlook. Brought up in a Christian home she was inclined to substitute religious duties for 'the one thing needful.' The question which she wanted me to answer was — What does it mean to be a converted Christian? Was it not living a good religious life? In a simple way I tried to illustrate the meaning of conversion by telling her the Biblical story of Rebecca. I remarked that the question which Abraham's servant addressed to Rebecca, the Holy Spirit, on a much higher plane, addresses to us: "Wilt thou go with this man?" I asked her if she was espoused to the Lord. Did she, as He commanded her, give Him her heart? Was her trust in the righteousness of Christ or in her own imagined goodness? Several months afterwards she called to see me. She seemed to be quite transformed in her conversation and disposition. She had asked the Lord to draw her to Himself; which prayer, I believe, He answered. The spiritual comfort which this new and spiritual change brought into her life she seemed to possess to the end.

God is able to save to the uttermost. He is the God of the eleventh hour. He can exert His saving power when our last breath is about to depart. Some who had travelled almost the whole way to "the last river" in a state of spiritual unconcern, He saved before the tie between soul and body was undone. This may happen only rarely; but it does happen. I hope I knew such a man. When I called to see him in his illness he was precariously sheltering in the broken covenant of creature merit. When I pleaded with him to throw away the soiled garment of his own imagined goodness, and to embrace 'the best robe' of Emmanuel's Righteousness, he seemed to resent the idea that nothing he was or could do, would ever bring him into God's favour. A few days later I called to see him again. "I have now," he quietly remarked, "no hope apart from the blood of Jesus Christ." On this safe and spotless pillow he now seemed to rest his sinful and weary soul. The mantle of peace which fell on the company who, a few days afterwards, sat by his bed I took for a sign that all was well. God was among us and we could not but feel his calm joy as his earthly pilgrimage was nearing its end.

The great promise that if we cast our bread upon the waters it shall return to us after many days God honours in many ways. I once saw this promise coming, as it were, to life during one of my visits in a large congregation in the North. After one of our services a certain well known Christian woman asked me to meet two of her friends, one of whom I had seen before. The other I did not, at the moment, recognise. But it happened that a year or two before, I had spoken to her about the supreme duty of seeking the Lord in a day of grace. With regard to the other I did remember the summer day, on my way to a church, when I quoted a verse of Scripture which had evidently taken deep root in her mind.

The Lord, Who often moves in a mysterious way, provided me once with another striking instance of His sovereign power in the salvation of souls. A Ross-shire lady was once in a hospital in Inverness. When I called to see her she mentioned another lady 'from the West' who was ill in another room. There I met a somewhat sad-looking woman with whom I prayed. When I spoke to her about the love which Christ manifested towards perishing sinners in dying for them she was deeply affected. Several years afterwards I visited a certain parish. The person with whom I stayed mentioned the name of a local lady who had expressed a wish to see me again. I was surprised to learn that she was the same one I had met some years before in Inverness. The strange thing was that on that very morning she had dreamt that I had visited her home and warned her against ignoring 'the offer of the Gospel,' which she was to receive that day. And, I sincerely hope, she did not ignore it. My unexpected arrival at her door on the same day surprised and startled her. She believed that God had led me to her door that day.

Another incident which deeply impressed me was that of meeting on the same street in a certain town — and within a few days of each other — a young man and an older woman, who both stopped to speak to me. In the course of our conversation the woman told me about an early morning in Glasgow when I appeared to her also in a dream and asked her to read Psalm One Hundred and Twelve. This Psalm speaks of the kindness of the Redeemer who "dispersed abroad" His unsearchable spiritual riches to "give to the poor." On awakening she read the Psalm which the Holy Spirit deeply impressed on her mind.

The following night she dreamt again that I stood in her presence and earnestly exhorted her to read a passage from the Gospel according to John. This she did, wondering in her own mind what these things should mean. On the following Lord's day she went to one of our Church services at which the congregation sang the Psalm, and during which I read the words which, in her night vision, I had asked her to read from the Gospel. From that day she began to seek "the Kingdom which fadeth not away." Her death, which came unexpectedly, was marked by great nearness to the Lord, and by the exercise of that hope "which maketh not ashamed."

The man also had his story to tell. It was that of meeting me some years before, after a Gospel service; but of this contact with him I had no recollection at all. The question I then asked him was: "Are you still clad in the garments of your guilt and sin?" The words led him to the Throne of grace where he asked the merciful One to remove these soiled garments from his soul and to clothe him in "the best robe," of Christ's Righteousness and Salvation. And God heard his prayer. Afterwards this man became a useful office-bearer in the Church of Christ.

It was while on a holiday in a certain place that I met two young persons in the way. They had been at our church service on the Sabbath evening, and when I met them later in the week I quietly introduced the urgent subject of their personal salvation. When I had spoken the brief but earnest word the one said to the other: "How wonderful that the Lord should now answer our prayer! For long we have been hoping that someone would explain to us these things." In much tenderness of heart they both bowed their heads as they willingly, I believe, received God's unspeakable gift. Throughout the years I have known them since then, they both gave evidence that they were truly the children of the Day.

I give these few examples out of many others that one could mention only to show how God in His sovereign wisdom can bless the casual word spoken in such a simple way. Many of God's servants could tell similar stories of God's Saving Grace in the conversion of sinners. Only the Day shall declare that His word, sown besides all waters and in all seasons, shall not return to Him void. This promise should encourage us to use wisely our opportunities that by all means we might save some. It would, however, be wrong to say that our exhortations are always welcome or always bear fruit. Our well-intended words often perish on the rock of indifference or unbelief. It would be difficult to describe all those types of people who tamper with God's grace and who by their sin bring eternal ruin on themselves. There are those who resent being reminded of their sin, and who count the great things of God's grace as "a very small thing." Some take up a frivolous attitude to their own spiritual state. Many are so preoccupied with their earthly affairs that they have no time to think of heaven, far less to prepare for it. Some procrastinate till they find themselves standing in the fierce glare of eternity with the precious gift of time for ever gone. Some convert God's sovereign decree in relation to their destiny into a pillow on which they lie to the end of their days. It is the old, old story: "And some believed the things which were spoken, and some believed not."

I should not like to end this chapter without acknowledging God's goodness in, I hope, hearing my prayers on behalf of some of my own offspring. There is a deep spiritual pathos at the heart of Queen Esther's prayer: 'Let my life be given me at my petition, and my people at my request,' which every Christian parent must have felt. There was a memorable hour in my life when the Lord met me in these words: 'But the mercy of the Lord is from everlasting to everlasting upon them that fear Him, and His righteousness unto children's children' (Psalm 103). On the day when the Lord shall bring all His people Home I hope to see there some of those for whose salvation I found it such a pleasant task to pray on earth.

Nor can I ever forget the day when, during a season of prayer, the thought gripped my soul that I should ask the Lord that as He had, in His mercy, preserved a Christian witness in our family relationships for several generations in the past, He should continue the same great favour in the years to come. For this I wrestled with the Lord till my mind was directed to words in Isaiah, Chapter 44: 'I will pour my spirit upon thy seed and my blessing upon thine offspring . . . One shall say, I am the Lord's; and another shall call himself by the mane of Jacob; and another shall subscribe with his hand unto the Lord and surname himself by the name of Israel.'

My faith clings to this great promise, knowing that He who gave it shall honour it in His own time. To Him and to Him alone be all the glory; for we are as nothing, but He is the all and in all — the Prince of Peace.

Chapter Thirteen

STARS IN RETROSPECT

COMPARATIVELY FEW of those who cross our path on life's pilgrimage leave any lasting impression on our mind. Our innumerable contacts with fellow men are often casual and uneventful. There are, however, voices and occasions which linger on in the memory. Throughout the years I was privileged not only to meet but also to listen to many good men. Some of these I have mentioned already.

A man who commanded my youthful interest was Dr Stuart Holden of Portman Square, London. Dr Holden's happy and almost boyish disposition was enhanced by an unconscious charm of manner and deep humility. Once he addressed our College Theological Society. He took for his subject the "man bearing the pitcher of water," and of whom the Lord said to his disciples that they should follow him into the house. In this fertile incident Dr Holden saw a picture of a living Gospel ministry which bore the blessing of salvation to thirsty souls. There are men whose pitchers are dry since they know not the Living Well. Such men would never be followed by the spiritually poor and needy. But a genuinely called and converted ministry which proclaims the Good News of free salvation to men will ever be sought after. With such men God's people will make their spiritual home. Such, as I remember, was his theme, and no word could be more searching or appropriate among a group of young men preparing for the ministry of God's Word.

The Rev. John MacNeill also addressed our Society on a kindred theme. He spoke of the predicament of the disciples when in the desert they found themselves surrounded by a large multitude who were faint through lack of bread. His address on the immediate availability of the Living Bread and ample grace was very instructive. "They need not go away; give ye them to eat," were words which continue to be spoken by the Lord to those who feed His flock.

A well-known figure in the evangelical circles of my early days was Bishop Taylor Smith. Physically the bishop was an immense man. As a speaker he was simple, fresh and arresting. Dr Alexander Stewart was his fellow labourer at meetings which I once attended in a certain Church. The Doctor addressed the audience on the worth and dignity of personality, and remarked that the physical universe, though great in size, was destitute of the moral and spiritual qualities which dignify the soul of man, especially the soul as it is renewed by the Spirit of God. By way of illustration the Doctor looked round toward the massive and good natured bishop and remarked that no one would dream, for example, of making a just comparison between our good and worthy friend, the bishop, and one of our near Highland hills. The bishop smiled at this remark by his friend.

Mr Graham Scroggie, who occupied the Charlotte Street Baptist Chapel in Edinburgh, was one of the evangelical preachers of that city in my student days. A spare, erect figure, sharp of eye, and possessing a penetrating musical voice, Dr Scroggie could sustain the interest and attention of any audience. His homiletic habit of alliteration, however, was often forced, and his somewhat literal views related to our Lord's second coming could not but repel many Christian minds. But for persuasive appeal and quiet effectiveness he had few equals. Two sermons of his stand out vividly in my memory — one on the Christian duty of joyously bearing the willow with the palm, or of enduring trial along with "the peace of God that passeth all understanding." (Lev. 23). The other sermon was on Samson's lapse and restoration.

There was another well-known Baptist minister — Dr. T. Shields of Toronto — whom I heard in Glasgow. His subject was the authority and indestructibility of the Bible, which he based on the words of the Psalmist: "Thy word is forever settled in the Heavens." "Should it happen that every Bible was destroyed, every recollection of it erased from the memory of men, and every allusion to its contents removed from all literature and art, would that mean that the Bible had ceased to be? No; for the Great Original is in Heaven. The Lord has magnified His Word above all His Name." These, as nearly as I can remember, were his words.

Another impresssive preacher who moved among us in those days was the then young Dr. Martyn Lloyd-Jones of Westminster Chapel, London. Dr. Jones was a precise theologian and an excellent apologist. In the delivery of his message he had drive and sometimes an impresssive and dramatic gesture. His balanced Scriptural Calvinism marked him out as a man in the Spurgeonic tradition, and his theological level was above that of his good predecessor at Westminster Chapel, Dr. Campbell Morgan. Professor Duncan Blair of Glasgow University was invariably his yoke fellow when he visited Glasgow. The death of Dr. Blair at an early age was like the fading of a star which had gladdened our sky only for a brief hour. One of the most memorable and moving sermons I ever listened to was from Dr. Jones, when, in 1964, he visited my native Lewis and preached on Psalm 107 in the Stornoway Free Church.

The man who did more in his generation, however, than any other in exposing the essential and withering unbelief of theological modernism was the famous Professor Gresham Machen of Westminster College, Philadelphia. It was left to this able man to expose the utter intellectual and theological impoverishment of this negative movement. Emerging modernists, who glowed for a moment in the sparks of their own fire, found themselves limp and silent in his hands. His devastating arguments cut like swords through all the men of straw which peeped through the quite silly and still-born books of his opponents. Only once I heard Dr. Machen, but one could see that his great power lay not in his tongue but in his pen.

There are books which find their way to our shelves and to which we turn for quiet relaxation in moments of fatigue. Such books, while they may not nourish the soul, may help one to relax in moments of weariness. Dr. F. Boreham's books one may describe as such. As books they possess much literary merit. Their chief value lies in the author's power to clothe the commonplace in pleasing literary garments.

This attractive writer I heard once in our General Assembly. He was greatly pleased when the minister who introduced him said that there was at least one man present who had two "B's" in his bonnet: the one was Bunyan and the other Boreham.

Dr. Boreham's speech on that occasion was characteristic in its originality and freshness. He told the story of a certain small town whose water supply was rendered unpalatable because of a stubborn and noxious weed which defiled the supplying lake. The weed was cut out only to grow again in greater profusion. It was only when willow plants which were of contrary but wholesome qualities were made to grow by the banks of the lake that the evil weed died and the waters became wholesome and fresh. In other words, only the Gospel, and the diffusion of Christian influence, can save society from moral and spiritual stagnation. Only the plant of grace in the soul can destroy the evil of sin.

Dr. Boreham gave one the impression of a man who went through life with his eyes very wide open, and perhaps of a man who moved more on the horizontal than on the vertical plane. His theological insights, that is to say, were far behind his literary charms. He was a man of the plains; not of the mountains.

But for pulpit grace and ability one does not need to go to the ends of the earth. There are stars, which, though their orbits may be small, communicate comfort and light to the mourners in Zion in a way we have seldom experienced in those greater gatherings to which so many find their way. Some of my most cherished memories are associated with Highland Communion seasons. It was, for example, in a small Free Presbyterian congregation in Greenock that I once heard the Gospel preached in the undoubted unction of the Spirit. The Rev. Donald MacFarlane was in the pulpit. Though much enfeebled through old age his sermon that day on the love of Christ for His Bride deeply affected many present.

There was another day when I sat listening to the Rev. William Cameron of Resolis in a large Lewis congregation. His sermon on the imputed righteousness of Christ was a most powerful display of a doctrine which stands at the very centre of divine Revelation.

I have already referred to Professor J. R. MacKay. There were few in his generation who could compare with this good man both for theological depth and for sheer pulpit power. I frequently heard him during my college days, but his great powers were then on the wane. Once I heard him in my native Lewis where he preached a profound sermon on the words,

"Now a mediator is not a mediator of one, but God is one." Outside the church I met the quaint John Macdonald of Shawbost, one of our lay preachers. John spoke about the sermon. "When I was a boy," said John, "I used to chase the wild ducklings which abound on our moorland lochs in the summer. Just when I was sure I was about to catch one it would suddenly dive to rise again far beyond my reach out in the middle of the loch. That was exactly how I felt listening to the Professor this evening." Two days afterwards the Professor, however, preached a simple evangelical sermon on that sweetest of texts: "For God so loved the world that He gave His only begotten Son, that whosoever believeth in Him should not perish but have everlasting life." That sermon was in the best evangelical tradition. It contained a full, free and universal offer of salvation to the sinner through faith in Christ.

A ministerial colleague once confessed that the most impressive sermon he had ever listened to was from Professor Mackay in the earlier years of his ministry. It was on the exalted theme of the transitoriness of all created things and the everlastingness of God's righteousness and salvation. "Lift up your eyes to the Heavens, and look upon the earth beneath: for the Heavens shall vanish away like smoke, and the earth shall wax old like a garment, and they that dwell therein shall die in like manner; but My salvation shall be forever, and My righteousness shall not be abolished." (Is. 51)

Although I have already mentioned one or two sermons which I heard from the eloquent lips of Principal John Macleod, there were two other occasions when in preaching the Good News, he enjoyed unusual spiritual freedom. One of these was in our church in Glenmoriston on the Monday of a communion. His excellent wife had just passed away. The blissful hope of the final ingathering of God's people, in the land over which the shadow of death shall never rest, was his theme that day. It was based on the words: "And unto them that look for Him shall He appear the second time without sin unto salvation." (Hebs. 9). The next occasion was during the opening of our larger church in Partick, Glasgow. The large gathering of Christian friends who sat at his feet seemed, in his own words, "to draw him out." The sermon was on the words of Psalm 132 — "I shall satisfy her poor with bread."

In listening to him that evening one felt that this able man of God was truly a star apart.

A picturesque Highland figure of those days was Doctor Donald Munro of Ferintosh and Rogart. His deep attachment to the old ways and the old days was an outstanding feature of of the Doctor's character. In the pulpit he was lively, if, at times, somewhat hesitant. His sermons were always rich in evangelical content, and were often based on Scriptural figures and incidents ingeniously, but edifyingly, spiritualised. They were, for that very reason, sermons which one could not easily forget. His sermon, for example, on Noah's Ark on the Flood was typical of his frequent method of spiritualising his theme. The ark was the church in its three dimensions. The lower part was far beneath the waves, and those who lay there in darkness and slumber had no true awareness of where they were or how they were. These are they who were in the election of grace, or in the Church invisible, but who were still dead in trespass and sin till God would effectively call them into a state of grace. The spiritually quickened were those who belonged to the second dimension. They occupied the second deck or floor. These were they, on the other hand, who were aware of the storms by which they were surrounded and who, like the disciples of old, often feared that they might perish. And those who occupied the upper part of the ark were representative of those who were at rest in a better world, and whose storms were changed into an eternal calm. Not many would venture to deal with this theme in his way; but the good Doctor had a genius for making it all very real, and within the context of his illustration or type, the solemn truths with which he dealt were deeply impressed on the mind.

Once in Edinburgh I listened to Doctor Munro as he discoursed on the living water which Christ gives to His own people, and which, whatever trials they meet with here, shall be in them springing up to life everlasting. Appropriate to these words he told the story of a certain roadmaker who in in the very centre of the road he had so carefully planned found that a deep hidden spring was bubbling up its water. But this he would truly suppress. When by bulldozer and steam roller he thought he had succeeded in his efforts he was grieved to see, a day or two afterwards, the spring bubbling up again its water as merrily as if nothing had happened! The Doctor then enlarged on the way in which sin and Satan try to arrest and destroy God's life within the soul of man; but their efforts avail nothing since the life springing up within them in prayer, praise, and desire has its source in God Himself and can never, therefore, be destroyed. "All my well-springs are in Thee." Their very life is hid with Christ in God. Doctor Munro was a man greatly beloved by the people of God throughout his native Highlands.

I cannot but mention another memorable evening in August 1966 when, in the church at Ferintosh, I listened to a remarkable sermon from Professor John Murray, of Westminster College, on the words: "Come unto Me all ye who labour and are heavy laden, and I will give you rest." Although we all knew that Professor Murray was a theologian of great depth he came down that evening to the level of the youngest in the congregation. His chief emphasis was on the words — "Come unto ME." We do not come to Christ to get something but, primarily, to get Himself. We come not for something but to and for Someone. For He is the one in whom dwells all the fulness of life, salvation, rest, peace and joy. We come to Him who alone can save us, and whose heart is tender toward those who are out of the way. Our coming to Him as "our all and in all" implies the subordination and, by comparison, the rejection of all created things. "Whom have I in the Heavens but Thee, and there is none (or nothing) on earth that I desire beside Thee."

But time would fail me to mention others who were among the excellent of the earth, and who, after they had served their own generation, "fell asleep."

We should thank the great Head of the Church that all the stars are not in retrospect. The promise is, "A seed shall serve Him; it shall be accounted to the Lord for a generation." This is the hour when God's people everywhere should plead with God that He might call into His service "mighty men of valour" whose weapon in the conflict would be the "sword of the Lord and of Gideon," and whose witness for the Truth might shine like a clear light in the prevailing darkness of the times.

There were other "stars" which had faded from the sky long before my generation came on the scene, and whom I would have loved to have seen and to have heard. I would have loved, for example, to have heard Dr. John Macdonald preaching to the weeping multitude at the Burn of Ferintosh from the words: "Hearken, O daughter, and consider, and incline thine ear." (Ps. 45). I would have loved to have heard Big John MacRae trying to make himself heard in one of the "Bochims" of the Great Revival as he discoursed on the love of Christ which "passeth knowledge," and also to have listened to Mr Archibald Cook on his favourite text, — "And they that be wise shall shine as the brightness of the firmament, and they that turn many to righteousness as the stars for ever and ever." (Dan. 12). I would have liked to have heard Dr. John Kennedy on the words of Psalm 48 — "This God is our God for ever and ever; He will guide us even unto death," and, much more, to have heard C. H. Spurgeon on the everlastingness of God's covenant love. But as Spurgeon himself would sometimes say to his friends after conversing with them for an hour on the things of God, — "My brother, we shall have an eternity together to speak of these things."

Chapter Fourteen

A PEOPLE NEAR TO HIM

IF SOME of those whom I mentioned in the last chapter were remote from my personal acquaintance, there were others — though unknown to the world — in whose company I was much refreshed in my soul. But of these I can only mention a few.

I can still visualise the little company who sat in a manse in Sutherland on a Sabbath evening in the summer of 1954. The Communion services were over. The Lord had been among us. We were all quietly resting in the drawing-room when a minister present, who was also my life-long friend, suggested that each of us should tell the story of some fine hour in our life when the Lord gave us some special blessing, or made some fresh disclosure of His glory and love to our souls. He began the conversation himself by relating how during another Communion season in that very manse he had enjoyed unusual nearness to the Lord in secret prayer. God's love and presence were so real that he felt his soul drawn towards the gates of Heaven. Joy unspeakable and full of glory filled his soul. Like a man greatly embarrassed our friend at last reached the point when he could find no words in our earthly vocabulary that could describe that solemn hour. But we all understood.

The worthy lady, who, without any persuasion, continued the talk told us of the day when, in an attic in a house in Caithness, God adorned her soul in the best robe of Christ's perfect righteousness. Before that hour she had been resting on her own imagined goodness and spiritual attainments. Now, as she stood before God's mirror, she saw how soiled were her spiritual garments and how unsullied and glorious was that robe which Christ had prepared and purchased for her by His life and death. Her soul embraced the gift, and as she saw herself "in Christ" as her Righteousness a new, unending song was born in her heart. That day she could say for the first time: "I will greatly rejoice in the Lord, my soul shall be joyful in my God: for He hath clothed me with the garments of salvation, He hath covered me with the robe of righteousness." (Isa. 61, 10).

In the company there was a worthy elder from the neighbouring congregation of Dornoch. He was a man who had passed through many sorrows. Death had emptied his home of his loved one. He was now alone in the home where the voice of a loving wife had always welcomed him after the toil of the day. But a deeper sorrow had taken possession of his heart. He mourned over "the years which the locusts had eaten." With God's prophet he could not but cry: "O my leanness, my leanness." One day as he entered his lonely home he leaned over the fireplace and wept. "Lord", he said, "after all these years professing Thy name, what have I to show for it?" It was while he was still in this state of anguish that God comforted him in the words — "For my grace is sufficient for thee." With those words God, as it were, began to pour His grace into his soul until, overcome by His goodness, he cried: "Lord, it is more than I can bear. Withhold Thine hand." And with a sad wistful look at the others he said, "It was the wrong thing to say." He was afraid that God had taken him at his word and withdrawn the breast of consolation from his soul too soon.

We assured our dear friend that the Lord who loved him just gave him the needed drink which, as he told us, sustained his soul for many a day. These three friends, all of whom are now at their eternal rest with God, were the Rev. A. MacLeod of Nairn; Mrs H. MacKay of Lybster and Wick, and Mr. John MacKay of Embo in Sutherland.

I may mention another such occasion which still remains vivid and pleasant in the memory. It was in a manse in the Island of Lewis on the Monday after a Communion. The company on this occasion was much bigger. It included a goodly number of young people who had just begun to show an interest in spiritual things. A minister present, who possessed a good tenor voice began to sing in Gaelic one of those deeply moving spiritual songs which portray the love and the sufferings of our Lord. This was followed by a season of prayer and psalm singing during which the Lord was felt among us and blessed us with His grace. Some of the younger people were deeply affected by God's Word. One elderly lady present, in a quiet whisper, constantly blessed the Lord for His presence among us. Among those who prayed that afternoon was the excellent Donald Morrison from Eoropie, whose name I mentioned before. His prayer was a plea for the promised day when sinners shall be no more, and when the glory of the Lord shall cast its benign light over the whole earth. That afternoon some of us felt as if time had stood still and that we were brought into another dimension where, in the light of God's face, the everlasting present leaves the soul blissfully oblivious of both yesterday and tomorrow. That day I could say, "Lord, it is good for us to be here."

How often also does the Lord literally fulfil His promise that where two or three are gathered in His name He is there also. I was still a student when I was sent to the Island of Mull to preach for the Sabbath. All that I can now remember of that weekend so long ago centres round a home which I was, probably, asked to visit. Even now I seem to see the composed and joyous look on the faces of the two women present—a mother and her daughter. Before we separated we sang a Psalm. My deep love for Psalm 125 I can trace to that night. As we sang the verses from that inspired song I had a new and overwhelming insight into the love of Christ who, in His attributes, merits and intercession, encircles His people in every age. As I walked to my lodgings under a star-lit sky, I could not but bless the day I came to know Him. When, as I was told, this elect lady came to die, God's peaceful and holy presence removed all her fears. She died with the words of Psalm 34 on her lips. "The angel of the Lord encampeth round about them that fear him."

God's jewels are often found in places where their spiritual beauty is undiscerned. Like the flowers which bloom in the remote desert, there is no one near to admire their beauty or to inhale their wafted fragrance.

Once, for example, as I journeyed through the parish of Ferintosh, I turned aside to see a very old man from Wester Ross who lived under the care of a kindly Christian woman. I had not seen him before, and I had no knowledge of the kind of man he was. When I entered his room he was already speaking. But he was not speaking to me. He was praying. He was adoring the One whose name is "Wonderful". The Holy Child Jesus who is in the bosom of the Father and who, in the mysterious feebleness of our nature, was also in the bosom of a woman, was the theme of his audible meditation. The aged face, with its dim and almost unseeing eyes, was both patriarchal and primitive. It was also transfigured and benign.

Sitting by his bed, I felt that I was in the presence of someone to whom God was very real. This was no imitation. Here truly was a soul whose spiritual element was God, His Word, and the eternal world. In one sense he was not here at all. There was something communicated to my soul that day which I find difficult to describe. It was as if the curtain of time was momentarily withdrawn and I was given a glimpse of those who in other ages walked with God. Within a short time this good man was no longer an inhabitant of time. How often since then I wished that I had met him sooner.

During my years in Ross-shire I was favoured with the friendship of a true man of God whose Christian discernment and intelligence were on a high spiritual level. On one occasion, as I sat in his home, he told me of a remarkable season of much nearness to God with which he was favoured. It happened a few nights before then. After laying his head on the pillow, and while he was still awake, he became conscious of God's awesome but gracious presence both within him and around him. Not only so, but in a way that he could not understand, many precious and encouraging promises out of God's Word began to unfold themselves before his eyes. Amazed, and full of wonder at what his soul enjoyed, he walked about; but the blissful presence remained with him for the rest of the night.

Personally, I felt that such an hour might be a prelude to, or a preparation for, some coming trial. And so it was. Not long afterwards a dark cloud descended on his life which brought him into the depths of distress. But the anchor of his soul, fixed in the eternal Rock of Ages, remained steadfast and sure amid all the billows which passed over him. If on the one hand the waters of a full cup of affliction were wrung out to him he could still say with the Psalmist:

"Nevertheless continually,
Oh Lord, I am with Thee:
Thou dost me hold by my right hand,
And still upholdest me."

It was during one of my visits to the Outer Isles that I was privileged to lodge one night in the home of an excellent Christian woman. She was elderly and blind, but her spiritual tenderness gave warmth and dignity to her conversation. Sitting beside her, she began to relate some of the milestones which marked her spiritual pilgrimage. Among other things, she described a season of spiritual anxiety during which even her body had lost all its power through the distress which held her spirit as in a vice. But in that dark vale God strengthened her through the words: "For thou wilt light my candle: the Lord my God will enlighten my darkness." The light, indeed, which God lit in her soul that day was never extinguished. In that home in the village of Crossbost I could discern the first hints of a happy eternity emerging from the depths of the soul of one who truly loved her God.

In another village in the north I visited a home where I felt the Lord was present. An elderly woman sat by the fire. I was already aware of this lady's exceptional intellectual gifts and spiritual attainments, but I had never been much in her company. On this occasion "the fire burned" and she began to tell me of some of her days of communion with the Lord. She told me of one incident—"Whether in the body or out of the body" she could not tell — which deeply solemnised and encouraged her. She had been praying when, in her own words, she was suddenly lifted out of the body of death and humiliation into a state of inconceivable happiness. It was truly Heaven, for it could not belong to this world. She was so enraptured in her soul that she did not seem to have any awareness of time or of sin, or even of her own surroundings. God was all in all. When I questioned her about the duration of this enjoyment she said, "For me time had ceased to be." There is a heavenly flavour about such "surprises" as these; but since they are so rare and personal it is quite impossible to convey to others what is enjoyed.

An elder who was present at that service asked a blessing that afternoon in the manse as we sat down to dinner. It was an exclamation of wonder at the love and condescension of

Christ whose delights were from all Eternity with the sons of men, and Who rejoiced in the prospect of inhabiting this earth where He was to suffer and to die for His own.

Let me end my remarks by relating another treasured memory. It was that of visiting Mr. Ranald Fraser who died at Maryburgh in the autumn of 1963. Mr. Fraser was a choice minister of God. Before this, my last, visit to his home, my own soul was greatly encouraged and revived by the words which I quoted above — "For thou wilt light my candle: the Lord my God will enlighten my darkness." Mr. Fraser I found lying on a couch in a state of exhaustion and much pain. Before bidding him a fond and final farewell I quoted these words. It was then that he opened his eyes, and he began to tell me of a sermon on these very words he had once listened to in the Island of Skye. The preacher was the Rev. Alex MacRae of Portree, an able minister of the Free Presbyterian Church. The sermon seemed to surface from the depths of his memory, bringing with it the spiritual flavour of that evening long ago. We both sat still as the words took possession of our hearts and quickened us again in our hope and desire. As I turned away from his couch I felt I would never see him again till the shadows of death and separation had for ever passed away. Here we take leave the one of the other for a little while — till we meet in the place where we part no more. "But now, ye have sorrow, but I shall see you again, and your hearts shall rejoice, and your joy no man shall take from you."

God's own bosom is, however, the place above all others where the soul is supremely happy and at rest. When our anxieties and burdens become almost unbearable, He can wrap us up in the peace of eternity. One of the most distressing episodes in the life of David was when he had to flee from his own son and from the thousands who were bent on his destruction. But there, in some green hollow not far from the brook Kedron, he went quietly to sleep, aware of God's protecting presence and loving care. That was the night when he composed the Third Psalm. There is not a moment in our lives but we are kept by God's infinite power and surrounded by His loving angels and also by the prayers of His people. How often in the experience of the Lord's people has this "awareness" of God's care broken through every barrier of fear and anxiety which would distress them. Those who enjoy communion with God also enjoy communion with His people. It is a wonderful thought that at whatever hour we kneel before God in prayer, there are thousands of others with us who, among other things, bear one another's burdens at the Throne of Grace. Such prayers, like "pillars of smoke", fill the upper sanctuary with their fragrance. They are also the means by which "the communion of saints" is truly enjoyed and understood here on this earth.

Chapter Fifteen

A BETTER COUNTRY

FROM THAT memorable night, when the Lord gave me what I believe to have been a foretaste of the deep joys of the world to come, the promise of seeing the Lord's face in righteousness has been very pleasant to me. In the house of their pilgrimage the Lord provides His people with songs, one of the sweetest of which is their song of hope on their way home:

How lovely is thy dwelling place
O Lord of hosts to me.
The tabernacles of Thy grace,
How pleasant Lord they be!

There are no words, however, in our human vocabulary that can do justice to this glorious theme of describing Heaven. Those who have stood, even for a moment, on the fringe of that upper world "wherein dwelleth righteousness" have found themselves silent and embarrassed through their inability to convey to others what, by faith, their inner eyes had seen, their ears had heard, and their souls had enjoyed of God's favour.

The vivid and richly symbolic language which the Scripture uses in describing the wonders of the glories of Heaven suggests that it is the place of such deep and unfading beauty that, through the mist of our earthly life, we can only see it darkly as through a glass. And yet the Lord's people when they enter it shall be instantly able to adapt themselves to all its delights and blessedness. Grace on earth gives them the capacity to enjoy glory in Heaven. Glory is grace in perfection. They shall not come to a people strange of language, of nature, or of activity, but to a people and to God bound to them in the dearest and nearest of ties. Heaven is a place. It is also a state. But it is, supremely, the enjoyment of God for ever.

A living, spiritual faith is the grace by which we look at the heavenly world, or at the things which are not seen. As in the natural world the telescope brings within our ken stars which the unaided eye could never see, so faith is the spiritual glass through which we look at the things which are unseen and eternal. In this way Abraham and all his spiritual seed saw Christ's day through the ever-brightening vistas of prophetic time. They also saw by faith the city that has foundations — the dwelling place of the Great King. What they saw they greatly desired. These Divine disclosures so intimately related to "the great and precious promises" of God's Word were so entrancing, and filled them with such solid joy, that, in a real way, they became strangers and pilgrims in the earth. The earth with all its pale, impoverished pleasures, and earth-bound preoccupations, faded into insignificance compared with what they enjoyed through God's promise of better things to come.

To such men Heaven was not a remote abstraction, a cold ideal, or a matter of mere "religious" belief. It was something the power and reality of which had already taken possession of their spirits. The very substance of the things they hoped for was already found in their hearts. God gives His people a foretaste on earth of what they hope to possess in all its fulness by and by. The Bride of Christ, for example, is spoken of in the Song of Solomon as having milk and honey — the choice fare of Canaan — "under her tongue" while as yet she was journeying through the desert. Abraham, David, Paul, John, Samuel Rutherford, the two Marys — with untold thousands of others, many of whom are known only to God — could speak of those earnests and foretastes of God's unspeakable love which had gladdened their souls down here.

The Lord's people, therefore, who live in the higher spiritual dimension of conscious nearness to, and communion with, God are perfectly assured of the reality of Heaven. "We know and are sure, that this is the true God and eternal life." True Christian experience and enjoyment belong to a very real world.

The spiritual graces of love, joy, peace and hope assume more truly the complexion of Reality than any other experience or any other phase of consciousness related to this life.

Those whose souls are enriched by these graces and enjoyments long for a fuller realisation of God's presence. They are conscious of new desires after perfect holiness and more communion with God. These, indeed, are the token of their adoption, the pangs before the birth, the thirst before the drink. In the land of Beulah Bunyan's Christian fell sick with desire to be with Christ, and in response to his cry, reassuring voices were heard from the City above: "Say ye to the daughters of Zion, behold thy salvation cometh. Behold his reward is with him."

When the Scriptures speak of Heaven as a city "which has foundations" the meaning is that it is the eternal home of the redeemed. Our bodily existence on this tiny planet is momentary.

There is, however, "a great gulf" between mere existence and eternal life. The Godless exist in their lost condition. The just shall live. The one is wrapped in the shroud of eternal death. The other is adorned in life and immortality. The new and unfading quality of the life which God's people enjoy in Christ demands a new world "which is incorruptible, undefiled, and which fadeth not away." This life is unaffected by what we call bodily death. "If a man believe in Me", said our Lord, "though he were dead. yet shall he live, and I will raise him up on the last day." The separation of soul and body is only for a while. Christ died to redeem both. The bodies of God's people asleep in the grave are as much united to the Lord as their souls are in Heaven. In death the Lord gives His loved ones sleep. He wraps them up in His promise and love, and bids them, as it were, "Good night"; and in the morning, at the touch of His power, and by the music of His voice, He shall awake them out of that long sleep. The body shall then leave its temporary abode to join the soul in Heaven. In the resurrection, body and soul re-unite in the Lord within the bonds of everlasting life.

The reticence with which the Scriptures portray the glories of Heaven is infinitely wise, since, in the flesh, we could not receive a full revelation of this lovely and happy world. It is described as "a large place" and "a land of far distances". It is most spacious, providing ample room for a numberless multitude of men and angels. Only God knows the number of the stars. And only He knows the number of those who, in the light of His face, shall shine as the stars for ever and ever.

This world of glory is also a place of infinite variety. The earth, which is but God's footstool, is lovely because of the variety of its scenes and colours. No two flowers are alike. Each bird has its own song. The rainbow has all the rich beauty of colour. Nothing is uniform. All is variety. Even the stars differ in glory, and their songs — which reach the ear of God as they move in their appointed paths — have a music unknown to our dim perception here. If the natural world is, therefore, so wonderful, what must that land be where all bears the seal of unending perfection!

But Heaven has a more intimate and more endearing meaning still. It is, as we said, the Home of the Redeemed. As one after another of our dear friends in the Lord leave us, our life here becomes increasingly lonely, and we long to join them in the Home above. When we visit the place of our birth, and the scenes of our childhood, we find the place but not the home. The loved ones are gone. Their voices are silent. Their smiles and embraces are but a cherished memory. It is home no more. But Heaven knows nothing of such changes. There the ties are unbroken and eternal. There the Eternal Father shall dwell among us. There we shall see "face to face" our spiritual Bridegroom who redeemed us by His blood. There also we shall see our mystical Mother, the New Jerusalem, who by her ministry and travail brought us forth to God. There we shall see those blessed beings who kept watch over us as we passed through this world, who stood by our bed as we slept, and who tenderly carry us away to God when we cease to breathe. Many of our loved ones whom we knew here and who, by their sympathy, affection, companionship and prayers, cheered our spirits in this pained world, are also there. Heaven is Home, unbroken by change, undarkened by sorrow and unmarred by sin. In Christ, and born of the spirit, we are already in the heavenlies, and live in its suburbs. "Ye are come unto Mount Zion, and unto the city of the Living God." Only a narrow stream, and the feeble vapour of our breath, lie between us and its enjoyment.

The apostle John speaks of Heaven as a nightless world. He tells us that it is also a world without a sea. Whatever pathos or beauty we naturally associate with the night or with the sea, to him their absence meant that in that world of peace there is nothing to disturb or distress the inhabitant. In this world the sea is the scene of storms, the symbol of restlessness, a barrier of separation. Our journey Home is across the stormy sea of life. Here we maybe often in depths of trouble. Happy shall the day be when the desired haven comes into view and we enter the calm of eternal peace in and with God. The storm and the night often go together. There is the hour of Jacob's trouble, and of Job's anguish. What are the nights — often without a star — which fall on the believer here? There is, for example, the night of adverse providence when we say — "Against me are all these things." There is a night of desertion when with the Bride we mourn over an absent Lord. There are nights of temptation, loneliness, grief and fear. And there is the inevitable hour when we must go through the last dark vale of death. But "there is no night there." The shadows flee away. Night gives way to Day. "Thy sun shall no more go down and the years of thy mourning shall cease."

The joys of Heaven are as varied as they are perfect. They consist supremely in glorifying God and in the enjoyment of His blissful presence. The enjoyment of God will be eternally associated with the worship of God. The "Bethels" of God's people on earth were always linked with their private or public devotions. Therefore, they desire nothing in time or in eternity but that they might dwell in God's House "to behold the beauty of the Lord, and to inquire in His temple."

A question which has exercised the minds of many Bible students, and which lends itself to speculation, has to do with the "location" of Heaven. Some say that this earth, renewed and purified, is to be the home of the redeemed. No doubt the day will come when this earth shall, for a season, become a reflection of Heaven. God's word, we believe, anticipates such an age of blessedness for the Church of God here. But this shall be only a passing phase within the circle of time. This earth is never spoken of in the Word as the place where Christ (or God) is going to set His Throne. It is merely His footstool. This earth is too small a place for God in which to manifest His eternal glory. It is also too tiny a sphere to accommodate "the great congregation" who are to dwell in His presence for ever and ever.

Others believe that Heaven is at the centre of the universe — somewhere in the great astronomical unknown. But as the universe is formed, it has really no centre. Everything is moving or receding. All is relative. But as God's Word tells us, the eternal City of God has a stability unknown to the rest of the creation. "Lift up your eyes to the heavens, and look upon the earth beneath: for the heavens shall vanish away like smoke, and the earth shall wax old like a garment . . . . . but My salvation shall be forever, and My righteousness shall not be abolished." (Isaiah 51).

But we are not to think of this Heaven in terms of physical distance — "far, far away." It is near. Where God is, there is Heaven. And God can be here as well as there. Time and space mean nothing to the One who fills all things, and whose presence is always with His own people. The mystery of a residential Heaven being beyond the realm of creation, while at the same time we may, through our spiritual communion with the Lord, be there now, is something which enters into the essence of true Christian experience. Paul was in the third Heaven while he was still in this world of time. To the Hebrew mind the third Heaven was a place which lies beyond the creation. It is the *where* of the I AM, or the dwelling place of the Triune God. "That where I am there also ye may be." "This is none other but the house of God, and this is the gate of heaven" was the ecstatic utterance of Jacob when he awoke out of sleep to find himself in communion with God. The fact also that we can, in a momemt of time, transfer our affections, thoughts, prayers and desires far beyond all space into that blessed place where Christ dwells, means that when we breathe our last breath here, we are present with the Lord. Our spiritual selves are our real selves, and even our bodies, when re-united to our souls in the resurrection, shall come under these laws of immediate enjoyment and realisation. The moment we awake we shall be satisfied in God's likeness and in possession of our inheritance above.

The question of knowing one another in Heaven has unnecessarily perplexed some minds. This is a subject which I have touched on in my book — "In All Their Affliction."

While there is no direct affirmation of this fact in Scripture it is, as an obvious fact of rational existence, everywhere implied. Apart from the many and clear implications of Scripture the final proof of our mutual recognition in Heaven lies in the continuity and indestructibility of our personal identity. Whatever changes affect human personality in time, or beyond time, it must necessarily retain the peculiar identity with which God has so wonderfully endowed every member of the human race. The Church in Heaven shall appear in the likeness of her Lord, and yet every member of His mystical Body shall preserve his or her own individual likeness. We shall, therefore, know each other. God is the God of Abraham, of Isaac and of Jacob. He calls all His people by name. It is also of the nature of grace to integrate, elevate, purify and preserve our personality. In Heaven, therefore, all our faculties shall function at their highest level. Therefore, the powers of recollection and recognition shall be preserved, for these are essential aspects of man's nature. "We shall know even as we are known."

The Lord can also bless a whole multitude of His people by suddenly appearing in their midst and breathing upon their spirits with the warm breath of His own mouth. Can I ever forget that Sabbath in one of our Highland congregations when I awoke in the early morning with the words: "Thy people shall be willing in a day of thy power." It was a cloudless summer day. We were already singing our first psalm when those who had arrived from another congregation began to enter the church. An excellent elder was walking down to his seat when something happened. God's presence seemed to fill the church. His power gladdened our souls. All could say: "This is God's House." A Christian woman who was present on that occasion said to me several years afterwards that something sweet and solemn seemed to tarry in the place for many days.

And may we not say that, next to being with Christ, being with His people shall be one of the joys of Heaven. How often on earth we would have shared more of the companionship of many of the Lord's people. But eternal ages in converse with one another in the Lord shall more than compensate for the denials and the loneliness of this present hour.

O, what a place is this! A land without tears, without broken hearts or crushing burdens, and over which the shadow of death shall never fall. It is a place of smiles and songs where all hearts are one and all eyes are satisfied through the everlasting beholding of the Lord. There the inhabitant shall never say — "I am sick". Our happiness shall be everlasting because we stand in the Righteousness of Him who is the unchangeable God. There also the King is always in residence. His banner of love, unfurled amid the glories of Heaven, shall for ever be seen over His people. Only in Heaven with Christ shall the new man reach everlasting happiness. It is reserved for him there.